Morgan Dollar
8 & 7 Over 8
Tail Feather Story

by

Leroy Catlin Van Allen

Revised January 2006

VAM 9 Presentation Piece

VAM 41 7/8 Tail Feathers

Published by

Rare Coin Investments (RCI)
P.O. Box C
Ironia, NJ 07845

TABLE OF CONTENTS

MORGAN DOLLAR 8 & 7 OVER 8 TAIL FEATHER STORY

INTRODUCTION AND SUMMARY

The design of the Morgan silver dollars first struck in 1878 at the Philadelphia Mint had a spread eagle on the reverse with 8 tail feathers (TF). These 8 TF dies were used to strike coins in March and April of that year. As will be shown, there were three slightly different versions of the 8 TF design. The hubs of each of these 8 TF designs were never used alone to prepare the working dies. Instead, one hub design was impressed over another hub design on the working dies that struck the coins. All 8 TF and so-called 7/8 TF working dies show evidence of dual, tripled or quadrupled designs. They are designated as follows:

$$A^1/A^0$$
$$A^2/A^1/A^0$$
$$B^1/A^1/A^0 \text{ & } B^1/A^2/A^1/A^0$$

All 1878 P 8 TF Morgan dollars have a reverse type designation of A. The designs on these A hubs were derived from the Judd Pattern J-1550. Briefly, the three known sub-types of the **8 TF reverse A design** are:

A^0– Parallel arrow feathers, staggered back of arrow heads, full wreath leaves, I of In touching the top of eagle's right wing, A of AMERICA away from the eagle's left wing and nine olive leaves.

A^1– Same as A^0 except wider center olive leaf in central cluster, slightly longer and more pointed feather tips on lower outside part of eagles' right wing, slightly wider feathers at top of eagle's right wing and slightly increased distance from coin center of wreath and legend letters.

A^2– **Hooked** eagle's beak, I of In slightly away from wing, reduced size of wreath leaves and bow top, slightly increased length of feathers in lower part of left and right wing, altered very bottom feathers of wings, lowered top arrow head, and added berry at top of left wreath.

(*Note*: The first draft of this report in December 2003 used the 8 TF sub-type designations of A^1, A^2, & A^3. Since previous books on Morgan 8 TF varieties had used the A^1 and A^2 designations, those sub-types are retained for their respective die varieties in this revised report and the new third early 8 TF sub-type is designated A^0 to maintain consistency with previous literature.)

As will be shown, some of the 8 TF A design working dies had a new design 7 TF B design reverse hub, derived from Judd Pattern J-1550A, **impressed** over them causing the so-called 7 over 8 TF varieties. This **new 7 TF design** had two minor sub-types:

B^1– 7 TF, slightly different wreath and bow designs, I of In well away from wing, A of AMERICA touching wing, lined up back of arrow heads, reduced olive leaf size, parallel arrow feathers with **long** center arrow shaft or nock. Slight differences in wing feathers location and length. Used for 7/8 TF working dies modification and alone for some Philadelphia and branch mint working dies.

B^2– 7TF same as B^1 but **short** center arrow shaft end or nock flush with other shaft ends. This sub-type was used alone for impressing working dies.

Modifications to the 8 TF designs were made out of necessity because the Philadelphia Mint experienced early working die failure and unintentional removal of parts of the eagle design when the dies were polished. This was due to the excessive relief of some parts of the design requiring high striking pressures and the shallow relief on other design parts which tended to be removed when the dies were polished prior to being used. But these modifications to the 8 TF designs weren't entirely successful in eliminating the coining problems. So a modified 7 TF design with a new hub was made which solved some, but not all, the coining problems.

The design modifications to the 8 TF design were made by the engravers **cutting away** parts of the **raised** design on a hub and **cutting parts** of the incuse design **into** a die. **None** of the three **Morgan dollar patterns** were used to modify these 8 TF design working dies by re-hubbing since the **patterns had major design differences** that never showed up on the coins. Instead, there are numerous evidences that each new modified working hub was used to re-hub the previous design 8 TF working dies. The working dies with protruding tail feather ends should still be designated as 7 over 8 tail feathers or **7/8 TF** as they have been known for the **past 40 years**.

The sometimes **complex** but fascinating exploration of engraver George Morgan's struggles with the many problems and modifications with the initial Morgan dollar 8 tail feather design in 1878 is an **important** **chapter** of the Morgan dollar history. The following sections examine the causes of the various doubling on the first 8 TF designs used, the second 8 TF "dual hub" combinations and the so-called 7/8 TF working dies.

MORGAN DOLLAR PATTERN DESIGNS

The three Morgan dollar reverse patterns are shown in Figures 1, 2 & 3 and are designated as J-1550A/P-1723, J-1550/P-1727 & J-1552/P-1729 as listed in *United States Pattern, Experimental and Trial Pieces* by J. Hewitt Judd, 8th ed. 2003, Whitman Pub. and *United States Patterns and Related Issues* by Andrew W. Pollock III, 1994, Bowers & Merena Galleries.

First Reverse Pattern

The Judd J-1550A pattern has an eagle and arrows and olive branch with three olive leaves and 7 TF identical to that on the $10 gold pattern Judd J-1545. But the $10 gold pattern didn't have a wreath and the obverse had a slightly different Liberty head. The motto and legend letters were similar to that on the dollar pattern J-1550A. The $10 gold pattern dies were produced in August 1877. The Judd J-1550A pattern dollar reverse eagle was also on the 1877 half dollar patterns Judd J-1508 & 1510 with wreaths and inscription similar to J-1550A. The obverse of the half dollar pattern J-1508 had a Liberty head essentially the same as the Morgan dollar with similar stars and motto. J-1510 obverse had the same Liberty head and motto but without the stars. These half dollar pattern dies were finished in September 1877. Thus, the Morgan dollar reverse pattern J-1550A/P-1723 was the first Morgan dollar reverse pattern of 1878 since it was essentially a copy of the 1877 patterns with modifications of the date and denomination.

Six silver pattern dollars of each of the designs of both Morgan and Barber were forwarded to the Director of the Mint, Dr. Henry Richard Linderman, on December 3, 1877 and another 20 each in mid-December 1877. There were problems with these pattern dies as related by engraver George Morgan in a letter to the Director of the Mint, Linderman on January 1, 1878:

...three dies have broken in striking silver dollars, and of course I have had to prepare three others.

Morgan later altered the reverse design as described in his letter to Linderman on January 30, 1878:

I have the working hubs for the silver dollar now finished. While making these hubs I have taken care to reduce the relief in places where from the specimens already made I found it necessary.

I have also altered the eagle cutting away the wings from the legs and making a few other minor alterations...

Second Reverse Pattern

This second pattern design is J-1550 of Figure 2 with notches in the bottom of the wings, a slightly different wreath with different berries arrangement, more pointed arrow head rear, A in AMERICA separated from the eagle's wing, I of In touching top of eagle's right wing, 7 TF with right two separated instead of overlapping and parallel arrow feathers with long center shaft or nock. The two stars have flat tops instead of the pointed tops.

J-1550 is an entirely new hub using the modified eagle's lower wings, a slightly different wreath and slightly different legend letter positions. The eagle and wreaths were on separate design hubs which were each impressed into a master die. The legend and motto were then punched into the master die by hand. Compare the spacing between the letters in OF and ONE to see the difference of J-1550A and J-1550 in Figures 1 & 2. The master die could then be used to make the working hubs which, in turn, could be used to make working dies to strike the coins.

In mid-February, 1878, Director of the Mint, Linderman, made a visit to the Philadelphia Mint and instructed Morgan *...to make some slight modifications in the reverse die engraved by him for the silver dollar.* Morgan's letter to Linderman on February 22 stated:

...I made the alterations on the working hub, which was hardened on Monday last...

These alterations make the working hub for the reverse useless as a regular working hub. I can make a specimen die from it, by cutting a part of the work in the die.

The hub for the obverse is unaltered and can be used at anytime.

I have commenced two new working hubs which I trust will be ready for use on Wednesday or Thursday next. After these hubs are finished I presume that we can make the dies for use, in from seven to ten blows each...

On February 25 Morgan wrote Linderman:

Today I delivered to Superintendent Polock an impression in silver from the Dollar dies showing the alterations which I have made under your direction.

I shall be glad to hear from you as to whether I am to make these or any other alterations on the working hubs which I have now in hand.

These alterations are shown in the silver struck pattern J-1552 of Figure 3. It is an alteration of the J-1550 design with the width of the eagle's wings cut back, olive leaves number increased to nine small ones, the center arrow shaft end is flush with the other ends and the arrow heads are smaller. The reduction in the size of the wings and arrow heads could have been made by cutting on the hub but the olive leaf number alteration had to be made by cutting into a die. The number of eagle's tail feathers remained at seven.

On February 28 Morgan wrote to Linderman:

Today I saw Col. Snowden with an impression of the dollar after the last alterations. Col. Snowden thinks that the alterations to the eagle's head and neck, the olive branch and arrows are improvements. He is however inclined to agree with me that the wings have been cut down a <u>little</u> too much, more especially at the extremities which now appear rather thin and poor compared with what they were.

This is obviously the pattern J-1552 with the reduced width of the eagle's wings. Col. A. Louden Snowden was Superintendent of the Philadelphia Mint from 1879- 1885 and chief coiner there from 1866 to 1876. Thus, J-1552 is the third in the Morgan dollar pattern sequence. But it is not exactly like the reverse design used to strike the first Morgan dollar coins, nor are the previous patterns J-1550A & J-1550.

Linderman wrote the Superintendent of the Philadelphia Mint, James Pollack, on February 28 the day that Congress passed the Bland-Allison silver dollar bill authorizing their production:

...you will instruct Mr. Morgan to finish his new working hubs, showing the alterations, as speedily as practicable, and immediately thereafter you will cause working dies to be made in sufficient quantity to commence striking pieces as soon as possible after the bill may become a law...

Thus, there were further alterations to be made to the two reverse working hubs mentioned in Morgan's February 22 letter to Linderman. But there were no patterns made from these altered hubs and they were immediately pressed into service to make working dies to strike the Morgan dollar coins. Two working hubs were needed to prepare the large number of working dies that was anticipated would be required in order to coin two million silver dollars each month as specified by the Bland-Allison Act.

Figure 1 1877 Pattern J-1550A/P1723
Photo courtesy Heritage Rare Coin Galleries

Figure 2 1878 Pattern J-1550/P-1727
Photo courtesy USPatterns.com

Figure 3 1878 Pattern J-1552/P-1729
Photo courtesy USPatterns.com

FIRST 8 TAIL FEATHER DESIGNS USED

The first Morgan dollar was struck on March 11, 1878 and was a Van Allen– Mallis (VAM) 9 die variety as documented in the book: *Comprehensive Catalog and Encyclopedia of Morgan & Peace Dollars*, by Leroy C. Van Allen & A. George Mallis, 1992/1998 3rd & 4th Ed. (VAM book). This first dollar struck had an 8 tail feathers eagle design and the obverse had engraver George Morgan's incuse initial, M, at the base of the Liberty head neck. This 8 TF design was used on fourteen reverse working dies combined with the obverse design A^1 with incuse M, and later with an obverse design that had a raised designer's initial, M, with parallel bars, I^2.

Pattern Derivation

The first reverse design used to strike coins is shown in Figure 4 of a VAM 9 Presentation Piece. It was basically Judd Pattern J-1550 with the same wreath, motto and legend letters. Differences include the eagle's right wing cut down some, 8 tail feathers instead of 7, shorter center arrow shaft or nock, thicker upper eagle's beak, nine olive leaves instead of three but slightly different than Judd Pattern J-1552, and narrow arrow heads with the middle one slightly shortened.

The two reverse design working hubs used to prepare working dies that struck the 8 TF coins were made by altering the design of the J-1550 Morgan pattern. It was mentioned in Morgan's letter to Linderman on February 22 that two new working hubs were commenced at the same time that alterations had been made to a working hub as requested by Linderman which resulted in the J-1552 pattern. These two new working hubs were derived from the J-1550 pattern design and not the earlier J-1550A pattern design which had a different wreath and letter placement.

They were also not from the J-1552 pattern hub since it wasn't a complete design hub and the olive leaves and arrow heads are not the same as on the regular 8 TF design used for coinage as shown in Figure 5 for the VAM 14-3 die used for striking some 8 TF proof coins. Linderman hadn't approved the design alterations when the other two working hubs were already being prepared. It would have been easier for Morgan to cut away some of the wider eagle's wings on a hub with the raised design of J-1550 rather than cutting into the die made from the J-1552 design in order to widen the wings.

Making changes to the design by altering or preparing a new plaster design and then tracing an electroplated galvano (Plaster model coated with copper for strength.) in a reducing machine to prepare a master hub was a lengthy process as related in Morgan's January 1, 1878 letter to Linderman:

... Presuming that I could have the Machine at once, I could get the die finished in about four weeks, I calculate nine days for the reduction, six days finishing and nine days hubbing...

Figure 6 shows a photograph superposition of the 7 TF J-1552 pattern design over the regular coinage of 8 TF VAM 9 reverse design. The white outline at the edges of the wings shows the wider wings of the 8 TF design which would have had to be cut into a J-1552 design die.

Figure 7 shows a photograph superposition of the regular 8 TF VAM 9 reverse design over the J-1550 pattern design. The white outline shows at the edges of the wings where the J-1550 feather ends had to be cut back on the hub. This would have been easier and quicker than cutting into a die of the J-1552 pattern.

Regular Coinage Die Doubling

Examination of the 8 TF reverse of the VAM 9 first coins that were struck and other coins struck from different dies of this same 8 TF design reveal extensive doubling of the design in every case. The question is what kind of die doubling is it:

 1) From hub misalignment during the working die multiple hubbing process which causes a regular shift in some design elements.

 2) Dual hubs of slightly different design used in the hubbing process. This causes overlapping of the different design elements and shows to a different degree on each working die.

 3) From a doubled hub which causes the exact same doubling on each working die hubbed by it.

 4) From two or more hubs that have slightly different diameters of design elements from incorrect hardening or annealing process. This also can cause a regular shift in some design elements, usually in a radial direction.

Morgan's letter to Linderman on February 22 mentioned previously also states:

... I have commenced two new working hubs... After these hubs are finished I presume that we can make the dies for use, in from seven to ten blows each..

In making a large number of dies we cannot give more than one blow a day, so in ten days after the working hubs are finished we could begin to coin at Philadelphia...

From this letter, there were initially two 8 TF reverse working hubs. The design on the coins from the first sets of 8 TF working dies, VAMs 1 thru 17, show regular doubling in a radial direction that is a shadow outline of the legend letters and wreath leaves (See Figure 8). The doubling extent and location around the coin's periphery varies with each 8 TF die but it follows the letters and wreath leaves exactly. This shadow outline doubling was likely due to a slightly different diameter of the outer wreath and legend letters on the two working hubs. The location of the legend letters and the wreath design correspond to the pattern J-1550 and not J-1550A. The doubling was likely caused was from the hub hardening and annealing process which caused slightly different diameters of the design on the two hub faces.

The eagle's left wing, body, head, tail feathers, arrows and olive branch don't show any significant doubling on these first series of 8 TF dies which should have been doubled on some dies if there was significant hub misalignment during one of the hubbing steps. An exception is VAM 1 which has an over polished eagle's left wing in the center and was touched up in that area by strengthening some weak feathers that gave a doubling appearance. Another exception is VAM 8 which has doubling of the middle feathers of both wings, eagle's head, neck and some body feathers. (See Figures 9 & 10.) This is a case of hub misalignment between blows which caused a shadow outline of these design features.

Eagle's Right Wing Feathers

All of the 8 TF dies show re-engraved feathers between the lower inside edge of the wings and legs. The basining and polishing of the 8 TF dies eliminated some of the original feathers there because they were too shallow in the dies. This caused a gap between the wings and legs. So each die was touched up making them uniquely identifiable with these two to three added feathers on each side of the legs. See Figure 11 shows an example for VAM 15.

There is a regular shadow outline doubling of the inner feathers of the eagle's right wing on all dies except one. This is a dual hub type of doubling with slightly different placement of feathers. See Figure 12 for VAM 6 and Figure 13 for VAM 4 as examples. Figure 14 also shows fine tooling lines to strengthen these lower feathers to create a better looking die for the VAM 9 Presentation pieces. The doubling on these inner wing feathers is weak for VAM 1 and they have been touched up with engraving lines showing (See Figure 15). The exception for this doubling is VAM 14-3 which doesn't show doubling of these inner wing feathers (See Figure 16). This die was used to strike 8 TF proof coins and, as such, is a special die that was specially prepared to eliminate most of the die doubling. There are engraving lines on some of these lower inner wing feathers to strengthen them as shown in Figure 17.

All of these initial 8 TF dies also show doubling on the outside feather tips of the lower part of the eagle's right wing, except again for one die, VAM 14-3. The doubling doesn't follow the outline of the top image exactly on the lower five feather tips as shown in Figure 13. Rather, the underlying design tips are more pointed or narrower. That indicates a slightly different design and the doubling is likely due to one hub design over another. Figure 18 shows a shallow underlying design tips of VAM 6 whereas Figure 19 shows for VAM 2 full underlying tips with weak overlying tips. This was caused by differing strengths of the underling design impressed into the overlying design. Figure 17 shows the feather tips for VAM 14-3 which only show the pointed tips of the underlying design of the other dies.

At the top of the eagle's right wing are apparent doubling of some feathers of VAM 14-4 as shown in Figure 20 with a close-up photo of the doubling in Figure 21. Note that this apparent doubling doesn't follow exactly the edge of the overlying feather edges. They are of different widths along the edge and extend under some notches of the overlying feathers. This apparent doubling is slightly different in strength and extent of the underlying design for each 8 TF die as shown for some examples in Figures 22, 23, 24 & 25 for VAMs 6, 14, 14-2 & 16. So this is a case of a slightly different hub design over another hub design that varied slightly with the hubbing of each 8 TF design. It isn't a case of engraved areas of just one hub since the apparent doubling varies with each 8 TF die.

Again, the one exception to the wing top doubling is the proof die VAM 14-3 as shown in Figures 26 & 27. It shows primarily the underlying wider feathers without the apparent doubling and this has possibly been cleaned up a little in preparation for the striking of proof coins.

There are also some lines and faint image of the first tier of feather ends next to the doubled feather edges at the top of the eagle's left wing as shown in Figure 21. Apparently the top wing feathers were being made more narrow and slightly lengthened by cutting back this next tier of feather ends. These remnants of the feather ends show on all the initial 8 TF dies. This resulted in a jagged line of lower tier feather ends instead of a smooth curved line of the ends as shown in Figure 28 for the pattern J-1550A wing, which is the same as J-1550 shown in Figure 2. The apparently doubled feather end tips are not due to hub doubling or dual hub designs but are from engraving tooling of them.

Olive Leaves and Arrow Head Doubling

The middle leaf of the left three olive leaf cluster shows doubling on some of the initial 8 TF dies. The strongest doubling of this leaf shows on the A^{1}d reverse die of VAMs 6, 7, 14-5, 14-8 & 14-19 as shown in Figure 29 and the A^{1}j reverse die of VAM 14 shown in Figure 30. It is not a shadow outline of a shift of a hub during the hubbing operation.

Rather it is a wider leaf design under a narrower top leaf design of a dual hub type of doubling. This was first pointed out by Pete Bishal in his *78 Corner #7* in the September 1979 issue of the *Numismatic Error Collectors of America (NECA) Errorscope* monthly magazine. He cited this as an example of dual hub doubling and that the first 8 TF design used was actually a dual hub.

Most 8 TF dies only show a trace of the narrow olive leaf over the wide one as a faint line. Some examples are shown in Figure 31 for VAM 9 and Figure 32 for VAM 14-4. Several 8 TF dies don't show any doubling of the olive leaf such as VAMs 2, 8, 14-2 (& 14-15, 14-20 same die) and 14-3. See Figure 33 for the VAM 14-2 example. The extent of this doubling on the olive leaf depended upon the strength that the underlying wide leaf design hub was forced into the narrow leaf design die. This was also the case for the dual hub wing tips at the bottom and feather widths at the to of the eagle's right wing.

This initial 8 TF reverse also shows faint remains of the center arrow head shown in Figure 34 for VAM 17 which was used on the Judd J-1550 pattern. This was pointed out in Pete Bishal's article *Let the Feathers Fall Where They May #2,* in the Fall 1997 Special Report of *The Society of Silver Dollar Collectors.* There are slight notches to the left of the back of the center arrow head that are even with the back of the top and bottom arrow heads. This pattern arrow head wasn't completely removed by Morgan when he re-cut the middle arrow head further to the right and the top arrow head higher for the initial 8 TF reverse. It is not a re-hubbing of the 8 TF over the pattern J-1550 or vice versa since the different lower pattern top arrow head is not evident. (See Figure 2)

It should be noted that these initial 8 TF design arrow heads do not match exactly any of the three Morgan pattern arrow heads. As was shown in Figure 2, the pattern J-1550 had about the same lower arrow head but the middle arrow head is further left with more pointed left ends and the top arrow head is lower. The pattern J-1550A arrow heads shown in Figure 35 had less pointed rear of the arow heads, the middle arrow head is further left and the top arrow head is lower. The pattern J-1552 shown in Figure 36 has more pointed rear of the arrow heads and the middle arrow head is further left. The 8 TF design arrow heads were made by cutting away portions of the J-1550 pattern derived hub and adding detail by cutting into the J-1550 pattern derived die as were other design changes from the J-1550 pattern.

Initial 8 TF Die Doubling Conclusions

The initial 8 TF design dies of VAMs 1- 17 had an *amazing* combination of various types of doubling not seen on any of the later Morgan dollar designs. The previously identified types of design doubling are as follows:

- **Hub misalignment** in hubbing the working die, VAM 8, which caused regular shadow outline doubling of the eagle's left and right wing centers, head, neck and upper body feathers.
- **Dual hubs** with slight differences in design that caused overlapping design doubling of the eagle's right wing lower inside and outside feather tips and upper feathers plus the middle olive leaf of the left olive leaf cluster.
- **Radial direction doubling** of wreath leaves and legend letters from slightly different diameter peripheral design on the two hub faces from incorrect hardening or annealing process.
- **Remnants of design elements** not completely removed during engraving modifications that caused shallow design remains of feather tips in the upper feather tier of the eagle's right wing and shallow remains on the left side of the middle arrow head from the pattern J-1550.

In addition, all of these initial 8 TF design dies have **re-engraved** two or three feathers between the lower inside edge of the wings and legs making each die obviously unique.

These dual hubs were of basically the same 8 TF design with only very minor design differences in one olive lea and eagle's right top and lower wing feathers plus slightly different design periphery diameters. Two initial working hubs were mentioned in Morgan's correspondence. One of these hubs could not have been a Morgan pattern since the eagle's wing's were either wider or narrower, there were 7 tail feathers instead of 8 and the olive leaves were only three large ones or nine small ones in a slightly different design. All of these major differences would have been evident on the working dies if a pattern was used to hub them.

The many small changes made in the dollar reverse design in progressing from one pattern to the next and to the final 8 TF design used to strike the initial coins was made by Morgan by cutting away portions on a hub or adding items by cutting into a die.

This initial 8 TF reverse type was identified in the VAM book as A^1. But as it is evident, all working dies were from dual hubs, as pointed out by Pete Bishal, and they should now be designated as A^1/A^0. The A^2 reverse type designation is still reserved for the second dual hub combination documented in the VAM book and discussed in the nex section. Therefore, the added hub type identified in this section is designated as A^0 to avoid conflicts or confusion with the A^2 designation used in current books on the 1878 8 TF. (*Note* that the original draft of this report in December 2003 used the hub designations of A^1, A^2, & A^3 which should now be changed to A^0, A^1 & A^2 respectively.)

Neither the A^0 nor A^1 design has been seen alone on a working die. They always appear as dual hubbed dies. The VAM 14-3 working die used to strike proof 8 TF coins is the closest to being only the A^1 design with no doubling of the wing feathers or middle olive leaf in the left olive leaf cluster. But it still has slight doubling of the peripheral wreaths and legend letters, so it is an A^1/A^0 dual hub die.

The hub design with a lower relief on coins and slightly lower and wider tip of center leaf of the left three olive leaf cluster is designated as A^1 and the hub with the higher relief design on coins and olive leaf is designated as A^0. The rest of the doubled design with the higher relief is also from the A^0 hub and the lower relief shadow outline is from the A^1 hub.

Figure 4 1878 P VAM 9 Presentation Piece

Figure 5 1878 P VAM 14-3
Used to strike 1878 8 TF Proofs

Figure 6 Photo Superposition
J-1552 Pattern over VAM 9 A 8 TF
(VAM 9 is white outline)

Figure 8 VAM 5 Doubled Wreath & Letters

Figure 7 Photo Superposition
VAM 9 A 8 TF over J-1550 Pattern
(J-1550 is white outline)

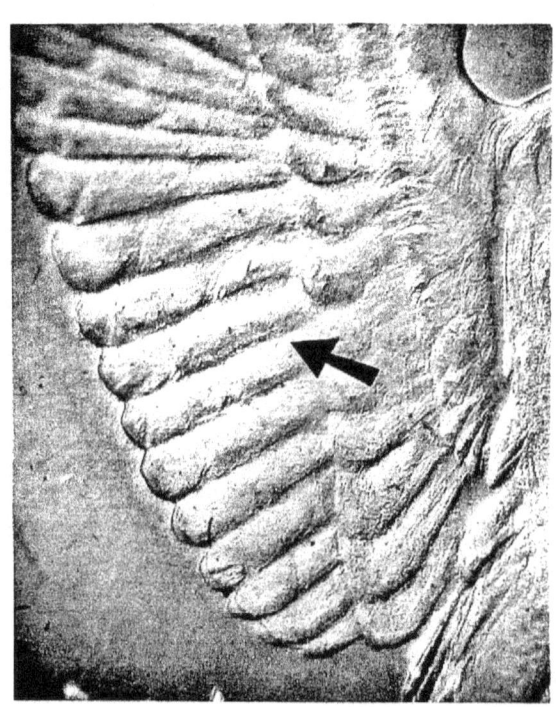

Figure 9 VAM 8 Doubled Wing Feathers

Figure 10 VAM 8 Doubled Wing Feathers

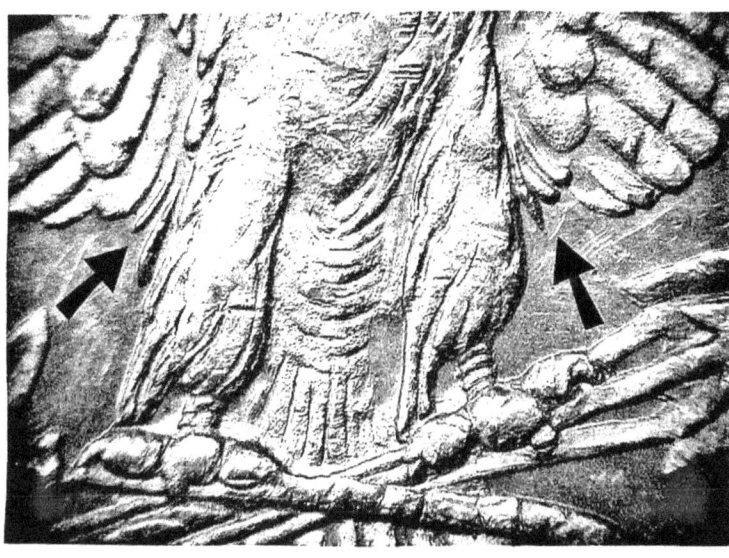

Figure 11 VAM 15 Engraved Wing Feathers

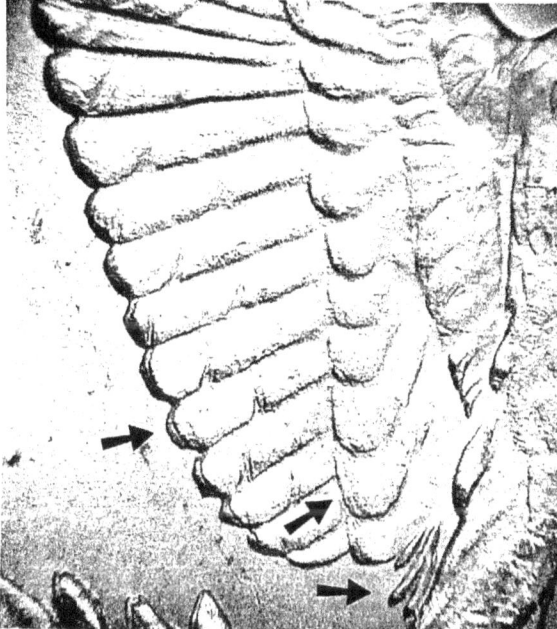

Figure 13 VAM 4
Doubled Inner
Feathers & Outer Tips

Figure 12 VAM 6 Doubled Inner Wing Feathers

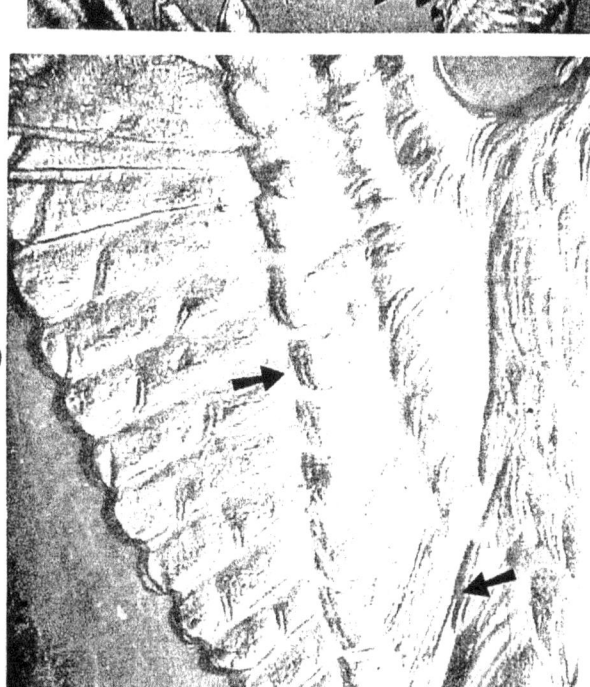

Figure 14 VAM 9
Doubled Inner
Feathers

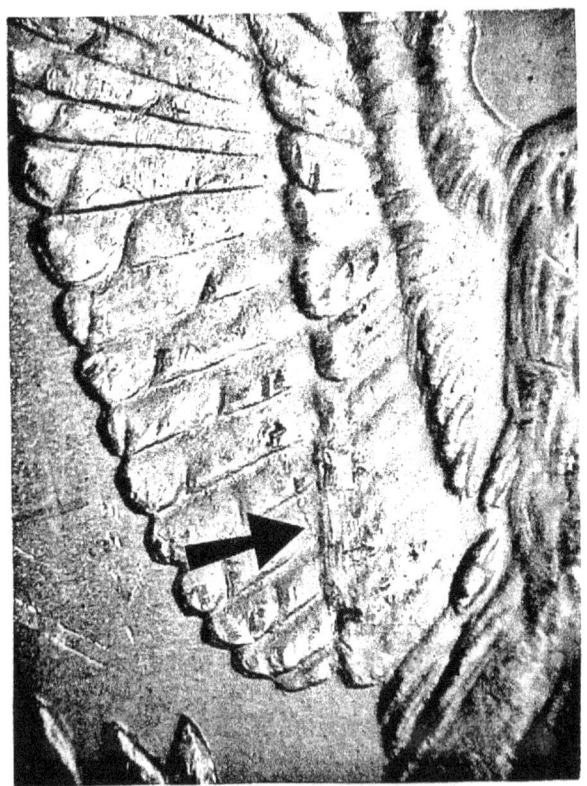

Figure 15 VAM 1 Doubled Inner Wing Feathers

Figure 17 VAM 14-3 Wing Outer Feather Tips
& Engraving Lines

Figure 16 VAM 14-3 Inner Wing Feathers

Figure 18 VAM 6 Wing Outer Feather Tips

Figure 19 VAM 2 Wing Outer Feather Tips

Figure 20 VAM 14-4 Engraved Lines

Figure 21 VAM 14-4 Engraved Lines

Figure 22 VAM 6 Doubled Top Wing Feathers

Figure 23 VAM 14 Doubled Top Wing Feathers

Figure 24 VAM 14-2 Doubled Top Wing Feathers

Figure 25 VAM 16 Doubled Top Wing Feathers

Figure 26 VAM 14-3 Cleaned Up Lines

Figure 27 VAM 14-3 Cleaned Up Lines

Figure 28 Pattern J-1550A Upper Wing Feathers

Figure 29 VAM 7 Doubled End Olive Leaf

Figure 30 VAM 14 Doubled End Olive Leaf

Figure 31 VAM 9 Doubled End Olive Leaf

Figure 32 VAM 14-4 Doubled End Olive Leaf

Figure 33 VAM 14-2 Olive Leaves

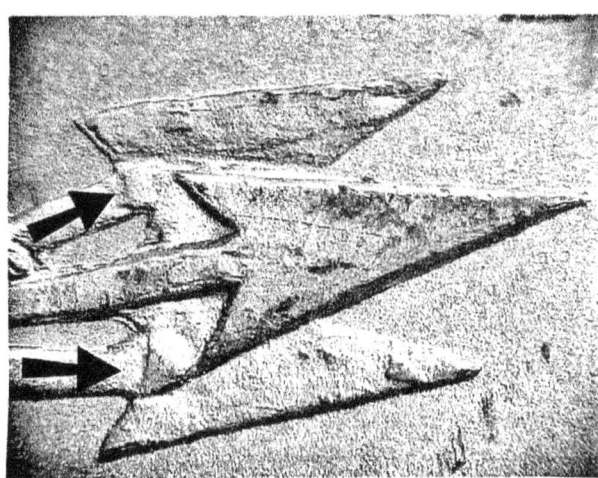

Figure 34 VAM 17 Middle Arrow Head Remnant

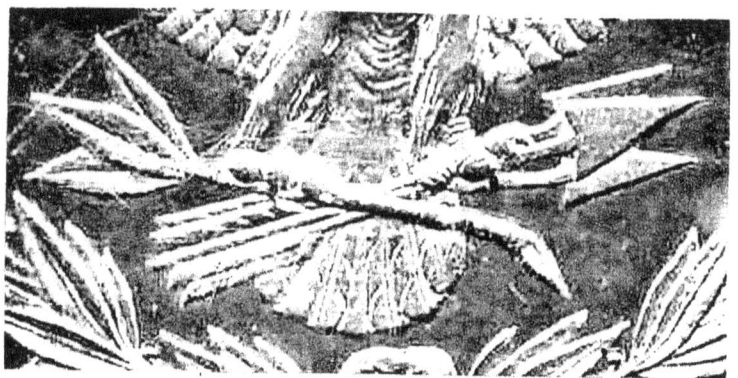

Figure 35 Pattern J-1550A Eagle Lower Portion

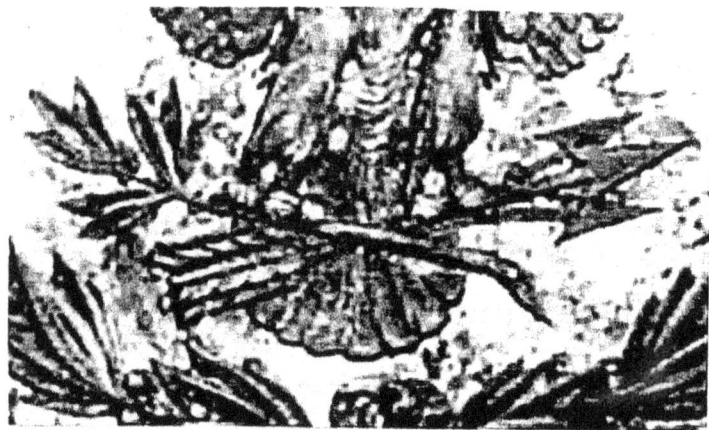

Figure 36 Pattern J-1552 Eagle Lower Portion

SECOND 8 TAIL FEATHER DUAL HUB COMBINATION

In January 1975 Bill Fivaz reported a dual hub 8 TF reverse type of doubling. It was discussed in Fivaz's *VAM CLUB-WITHIN-A CLUB REPORT #9* of the August 1976 issue of the *NECA Errorscope* monthly magazine. This dual hub is designated as A^2/A^1 in the VAM book. It is characterized by a doubled eagle's lower beak and a hooked upper beak plus the I of In is away from the eagle's wing. There is also variable doubling of the outside edges of the wings, top arrow head, wreath leaves and legend letters. Five different reverse dies of this second dual hub combination are known and are designated as VAMs 18 thru 23. (One listed reverse die variety is combined with two different obverse dies of VAMs 19 & 23.)

The initial 8 TF working dies (Identified in the previous section as a dual hub combination with new designation of A^1/A^0.) were difficult to properly basin (Lapping of the coin's field to produce a certain radius on the die face.) and resulted in the removal of some lower wing feathers. This required that an engraver touch up each die in these blank areas to cut into and add back some missing wing feathers. Each die was therefore slightly different in these areas. In an attempt to overcome these basining difficulties, Morgan modified the 8 TF design to create a third hub version, A^2. This third 8 TF version was then used to re-hub five of the earlier A^1/A^0 working dies. The extent that the design differences showed up on these five re-hubbed dies varied with the strength of the re-hubbing.

A^2 Hub Design Changes

There are numerous small changes in the A^2 design from the previously used A^1/A^0 initial dual hub design. As mentioned earlier, the eagle's beak was given a sharper hook in A^2 design (See Figure 37) for VAM 20 compared to that of the earlier A^1/A^0 beak (See Figure 38 for VAM 14-2). VAMs 20 & 21 show the A^2 beak, while VAMs 18, 19 (& 23 which has same reverse die) and 22 show doubling primarily on the lower beak which is different on each die (See Figure 39 for VAM 19). This indicates doubling due to a dual hub on working dies and not a doubled hub where a new design eagle's head was somehow impressed into a master die to cause a doubled hub.

The bottom edge of the eagle's right wing was modified by adding a feather between the wing and leg as shown in Figure 40 for VAM 19. Two small feathers were combined into one large one on the lower part of the eagle's left wing, a small feather was made slightly larger and one feather was eliminated. Compare these lower wing areas with that of the A^1/A^0 design shown in Figure 41 for VAM 5. Remnants of the A^1/A^0 lower feather design show on VAMs 18 and 22 at both left and right lower wing and leg area, as shown in Figure 42 for VAM 18.

There were some slight changes made to the olive on the olive branch from the A^1/A^0 design to the A^2 design. The A^1/A^0 olive has a larger olive on top of the branch next to the olive leaves and a large raised portion below the olive branch that is blunt on the left side as shown in Figure 41. The primarily A^2 design on VAMs 19 & 23 plus the other $A^2/A^1/A^0$ die varieties of VAMs 18, 20, 21 & 22 all have a small olive on top and a small oblong raised portion below that blends into the branch bottom on both sides as shown in Figures 40 & 42.

Moving down to the arrow heads, the shaft just behind the top arrow head is angled upwards from the middle arrow shaft on the A^1/A^0 reverse as was shown in Figure 34. The A^2 reverse has the top arrow shaft parallel with the middle arrow shaft (See Figure 43). Some of the second dual hub reverses show this top arrow head and shaft doubled (See Figure 44 for VAM 20) with the remnants of the A^1/A^0 top arrow head. The A^2 arrow heads are different than any of the three pattern ones, which were blunted backs of Judd J-1550A of Figure 35, even backs of Judd J-1550 of Figure 2 or very pointed and slightly staggered backs of Judd J-1552 of Figure 36.

Further down, the wreath bow was strengthened on the left side and the wreath leaf next to the upper left of the bow was cut back (See Figures 45, 46 & 47 for VAMs 7, 18 & 19). Some of the wreath leaves were also cut back and reduced in size on the A^2 reverse (See Figures 48, 49 & 50 for VAMs 14-2, 22 & 19). In the left wreath, the top left leaf of the second from top leaf cluster was eliminated and a berry and vertical branch put in its place. This was not just a polishing of the dies that reduced the leaf end lengths. There are overlapping end notches of the shorter leaves over the longer leaves in Figure 49. Figure 46 shows the overlapping of the side of a leaf next to the top left of the wreath bow.

The I of In no longer touches the wing edge on the second dual hub combination die varieties of VAMs 18- 23, as shown in Figure 51 for VAM 22. Compare the In vertical location for VAM 22 in Figure 51 to that of Figure 52 of VAM 17 of the A^1/A^0 design. The lower serifs of In were cut away making the bottom line of In higher than the bottom line of God which was even in the A^1/A^0 design of Figure 52. A wide over narrow G of God is shown in Figure 53 for VAM 21. The slightly wider outside and narrower inside space of the G in the A^1/A^0 design shown in Figure 52 than that of the A^2 design shown in Figure 51.

The eagle's right wing was widened all along it's edge by slightly lengthening the feathers on the A^2 type reverse. This resulted in doubling of the wing edges when the A^2 hub was impressed over the A^1/A^0 design dies as shown in Figure 54 for VAM 20. The A^1/A^0 eagle's right wing is shown in Figure 55 for VAM 7 and the basically A^2 design with little doubling is shown in Figure 56 for VAM 19. VAMs 18, 21 & 22 also show some doubling of this wing edge with file lines along the doubling in an attempt to smooth it out. The wider A^2 wing design is at a lower level than the narrower A^1/A^0 design. This doubling is much wider and over a longer wing length than the doubling previously shown in Figure 13 for the A^1/A^0 wing. The eagle's right wing width of the A^2 design is still not as wide as the J-1550 pattern wing as shown in Figure 57 photo superposition. The increased width of the A^2 wing design compared to the A^1/A^0 wing is shown in a photo superposition in Figure 58. The increased width of these wing feathers can also be seen by comparing the tip lengths from some of the feather notches shown in Figures 55 & 56.

The eagle's left wing was also slightly widened on the lower edge by lengthening the feathers. This also resulted in slight doubling of this edge as shown in Figure 59 for VAM 20. The slight lengthening of the wing tips can best be shown by comparing the tip lengths from some of the feather notches as shown in Figure 60 for A^1/A^0 design of VAM 6 and Figure 61 for the A^2 design of VAM 19.

As further proof that the later A^2 design hub was entered into A^1/A^0 working dies, Figure 62 of VAM 20 shows the same type of feather edge doubling at the top of the eagle's right wing as was shown for VAMs 6, 14 & 16 in Figures 22, 23 & 25. This same wing area shown in Figure 63 of VAM 19 is mostly A^2 design and doesn't show the doubling of the feather edge. There is the same jagged feather ends of the first tier from the wing top however as the A^1/A^0 design shown in Figures 22, 23 & 25.

To accomplish these various small design changes for the A^2 reverse, Morgan removed details on one of the earlier A design hubs by cutting them away in places and strengthened details by cutting them into a die. He couldn't have used any of the pattern hubs to impress directly into the A^1/A^0 working dies since the eagle, arrow heads and olive leaves all had significant design differences which are not apparent on any of these second dual hub 8TF dies.

Second 8 TF Series Die Doubling Conclusions

The five 8 TF reverse varieties of VAMs 18-23, with one common reverse (VAMs 19 & 23) with different obverse dies, are designated as A^2/A^1 dual hubs in the VAM book. The most notable die doubling feature on these second 8 TF reverse variety series is a doubled eagle's beak that is more hooked at the end than the initial 8 TF reverse die series. This indicates a possible dual hub since the doubling of the eagle's beak varies with each of these reverse dies.

The feathers at the bottom of both eagle's wings next to the leg were modified and strengthened to overcome their disappearance in the initial A^1/A^0 8 TF design when the working dies were basined. However, some of the dies (VAMs 18 & 22) show remnants of the initial A^1/A^0 lower feather design indicating that they are actually $A^2/A^1/A^0$ hubbing.

There are remnants of the top arrow shaft and head above that of these five reverse dies. The A^2 top arrow shaft and head was lowered but the remains of the A^1/A^0 ones still show above it. None of the Morgan pattern arrow heads match the A^2 design.

In the left wreath of the A^2 design, the top left leaf of the second from top leaf cluster was eliminated and a berry and vertical branch put in it's place. These five reverse dies show various stages of the A^2 over A^1/A^0 design in this area as well as around the wreath bow.

Both eagle's wings were slightly widened on the lower part and show doubling near the tips that matches the underlying narrow A^1/A^0 wing design.

Some of the A^2 reverse dies show the same doubling at the top of the eagle's right wing as the A^1/A^0 dies and all show the jagged ends of the first tier of feather ends in the eagle's right wing that are only on the A^1/A^0 dies and not on the three pattern designs.

These various doubling in the eagle's wings, top arrow shaft and head, top of left wreath and wreath bow match the A^1/A^0 design as the underlying one.

The A^2 design is a modification of the A^0 and A^1 hub designs but it wasn't used alone to hub working dies. The five second 8 TF reverse working dies series are actually the A^2 design hubbed over the A^1/A^0 working dies or a triple hubbing of $A^2/A^1/A^0$.

8 TF Reverse & Obverse Die Combinations/Possible Sequences

The 19 8 TF reverse dies were used with different obverse design types as described in the VAM book. Specific obverse and reverse die combinations can be difficult to attribute because of small differences in the engraved feathers between the wings and legs, extensive doubling of many design features and pairing of some reverse dies with multiple obverse dies. This 8 TF coin attribution is made relatively easy in the useful book *1878 Morgan Dollar 8-TF Attribution Guide* by Jeff Oxman & Les Hartnett, 3rd ed., 2004 with detailed close-up photos of each coin variety and charts to help identify them.

There are two obverse sub-types used with most of the 8 TF reverse dies: I^1 with incuse designer's initial M shown in Figure 64 for VAM 3 and I^2 with raised designer's initial M shown in Figure 65 for VAM 1. Additional detail differences are described in the VAM book. Also, some of the 8 TF reverse dies were paired with dual hub obverse dies, II/I, which were a later second obverse design hubbed over the first I obverse design working dies. These II/I obverse dies are characterized by a short pointed inner ear fill and thick doubled LIBERTY letters shown in Figures 66 & 67 for VAMs 16. This is compared to a long more blunted ear fill and thin LIBERTY letters of the I obverse shown in Figure 68 for VAM 10 and Figure 69 for VAM 14-1. Figures 70 & 71 show the ear and LIBERTY of the II design for VAM 195. Additional details of these II/I dual hub obverses are given in the VAM book.

The 19 8 TF reverse dies combined with obverse dies are given below. The VAM book listings of VAMs 11 & 13 was later determined that their die combinations don't exist. The possible die sequences of a particular reverse die with multiple obverse dies is provided by Michael S. Fey and William Finelli. (*Note*: VAM book reverse designations are used: A^1 is actually A^1/A^0 and A^2/A^1 is actually $A^2/A^1/A^0$.)

A^1a– $I^2$1 (VAM 1)

A^1b– $I^2$2 (VAM 2)

A^1c– $I^1$1 (VAM 3), $I^2$3 (VAM 4), $I^2$4 (VAM 5), $I^1$6 (VAM 14-6), $I^1$7 (VAM 14-7), $I^1$11 (VAM 14-11), $I^1$12 (VAM 14-12), $I^1$14 (VAM 14-14), $I^1$16 VAM 14-17), $I^1$17 (VAM 14-18)

    A^1c possible sequence: 14-17, 14-18, 14-12, 14-14, 14-7, 3, 14-6, 14-11, 4, 5

    (*Note*: **Amazing** nine obverse dies combined with this one reverse die!! Die sequence subject to change as die cracks only appear at ME in AMERICA on last few die combinations; VAM 5 possibly before VAM 4.)

A^1d– $I^2$5 (VAM 6), $I^2$6 (VAM 7), $I^2$10 (VAM 14-5), $I^1$8 (VAM 14-8 Proof), $I^1$18 (VAM 14-19)

    A^1d possible die sequence: 14-8 Proof, 14-19, 6, 14-5, 7

A^1e– $I^2$8 (VAM 10), II/I 1 (VAM 15) A^1e possible die sequence: 15, 10

A^1f– $I^2$9 (VAM 12), II/I 4 (VAM 16), II/I 5 (VAM 17)

    A^1f possible die sequence: 12, 16, 17 (Van Allen die sequence)

A^1g– $I^2$7 (VAM 8)

A^1h– $I^1$2 (VAM 9 Presentation)

A^1i– $I^2$2 (VAM 14-4)

A^1j– $I^1$2 (VAM 14)

A^1k– $I^1$3 (VAM 14-1), $I^1$5 (VAM 14-10) A^1k possible die sequence: 14-10, 14-1

A^1l– $I^1$4 (VAM 14-2), $I^1$2 (VAM 14-15), $I^1$19 (VAM 14-20)

    A^1l possible die sequence: 14-15, 14-20, 14-2

A^1m– $I^1$5 (VAM 14-3 Proof)

A^1n– $I^1$9 (VAM 14-9), $I^1$13 (VAM 14-13), $I^1$15 (VAM 14-16)

    A^1n possible die sequence: 14-13, 14-16, 14-9

A^2/A^1a– II/I 2 (VAM 18)

A^2/A^1b– II/I 2 (VAM 19), $I^2$11 (VAM 23) A^2/A^1b possible die sequence: 23, 19

A^2/A^1c– II/I 2 (VAM 20)

A^2/A^1d– II/I 3 (VAM 21)

A^2/A^1e– II/I 6 (VAM 22)

Possible obverse die sequences:

    $I^1$2: 9, 14, 14-15 (Jeff Oxman die sequence)

    $I^1$5: 14-3, 14-10 (Jeff Oxman die sequence)

    $I^2$2: 2, 14-4 (Jeff Oxman die sequence)

    II/I 2: 19, 18, 20 (Jeff Oxman die sequence)

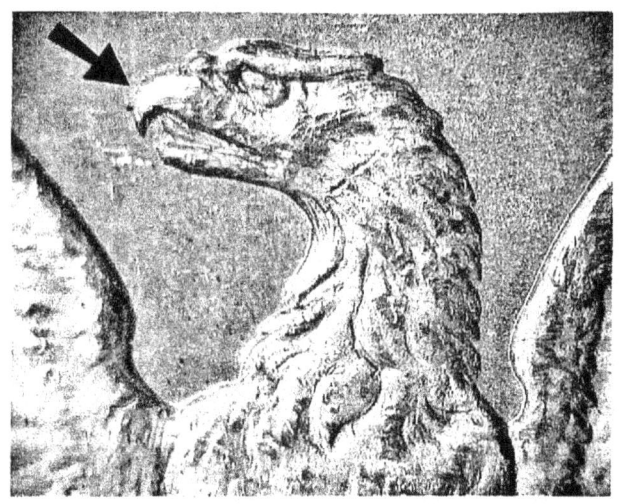

Figure 37 VAM 20 A^2 Eagle's Head

Figure 38 VAM 14-2 A^1/A^0 Eagle's Head

Figure 39 VAM 19 A^2/A^1/A^0 Eagle's Head

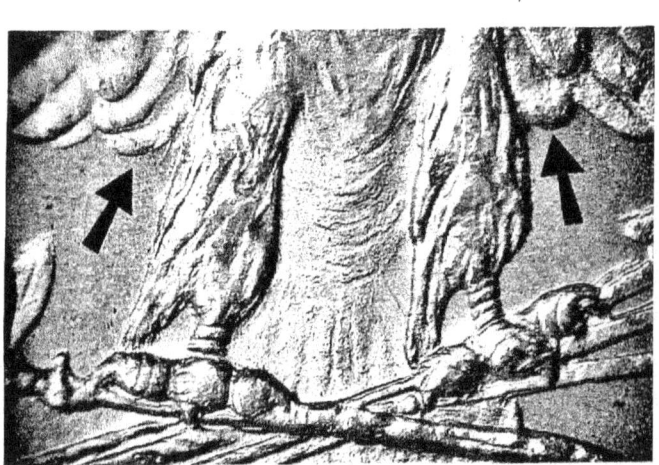

Figure 40 VAM 19 A^2 Bottom of Wings

Figure 41 VAM 5 A^1/A^0 Bottom of Wings

Figure 42 VAM 18 A^2/A^1/A^0 Bottom of Wings

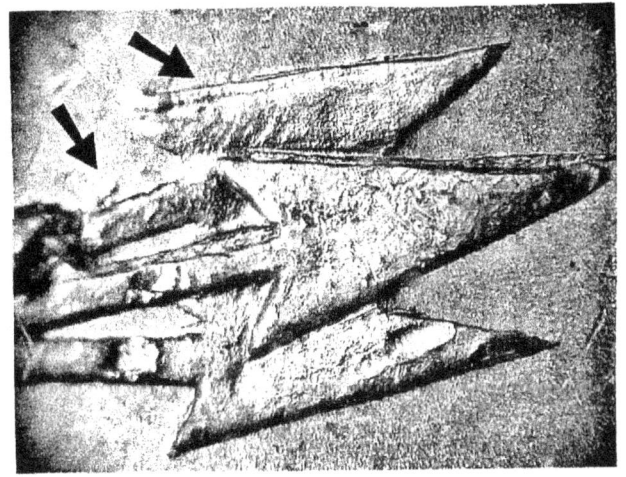

Figure 43 VAM 22 A^2 Arrow Heads

Figure 44 VAM 20 $A^2/A^1/A^0$ Arrow Heads

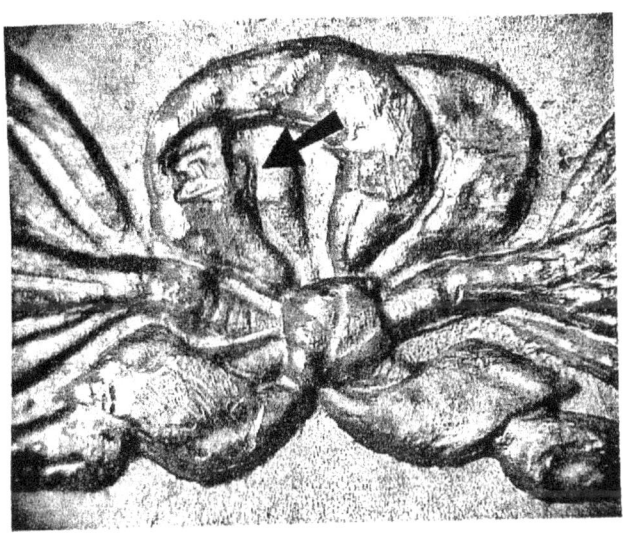

Figure 45 VAM 7 A^1/A^0 Wreath Bow

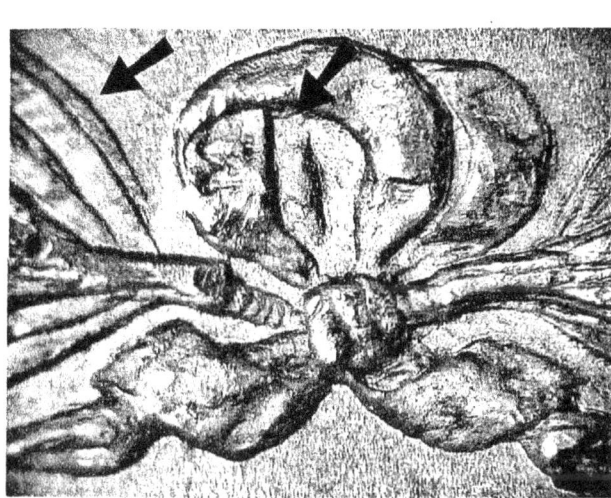

Figure 46 VAM 18 $A^2/A^1/A^0$ Wreath Bow

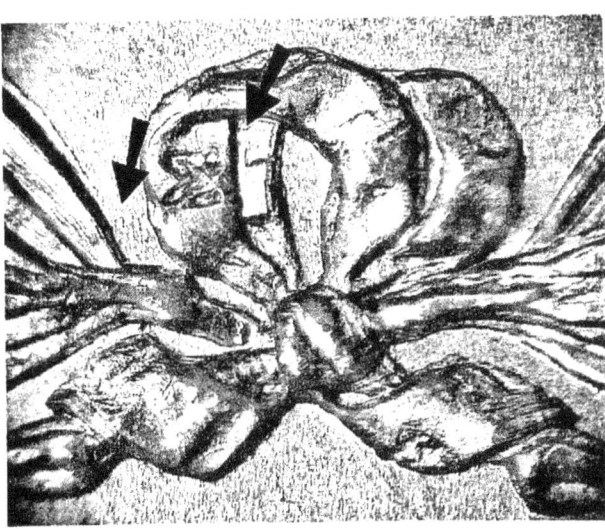

Figure 47 VAM 19 A^2 Wreath Bow

Figure 48 VAM 14-2 A^1/A^0
Left Wreath Top

Figure 49 VAM 22 A^2/A^1/A^0
Left Wreath Top

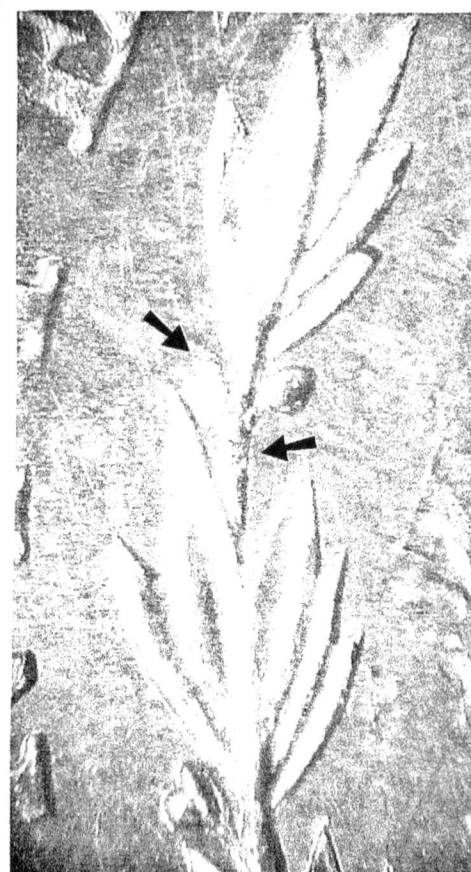

Figure 50 VAM 19 A^2
Left Wreath Top

Figure 51 VAM 22 In God We

Figure 52 VAM 17 In God We

Figure 53 VAM 21 Doubled G in God

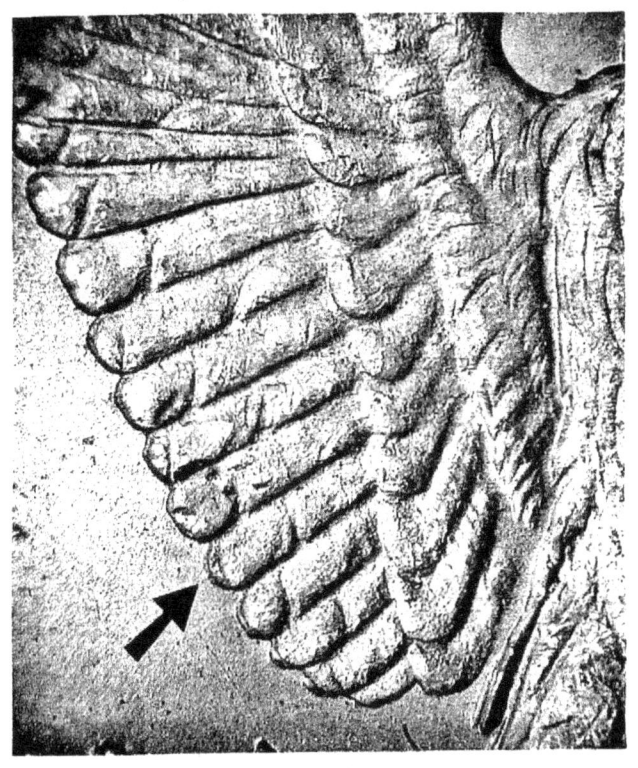

Figure 55 VAM 7 A^1/A^0 Eagle's Rt. Wing

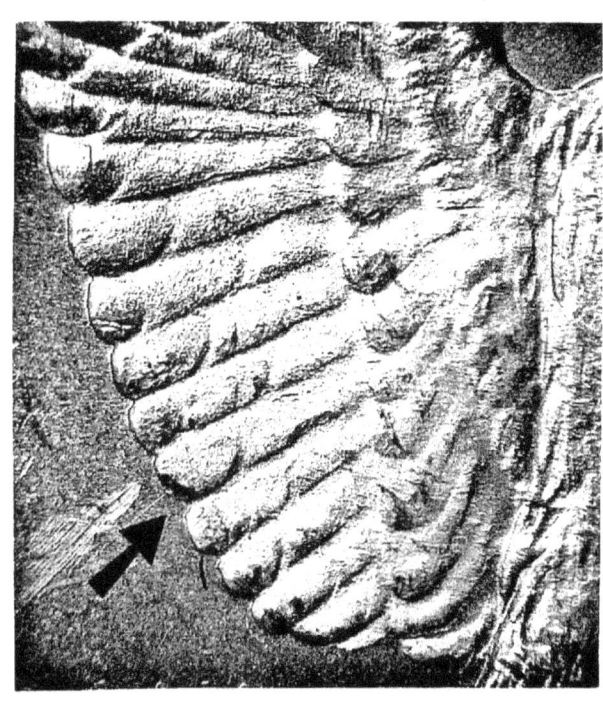

Figure 56 VAM 19 A^2 Eagle's Rt. Wing

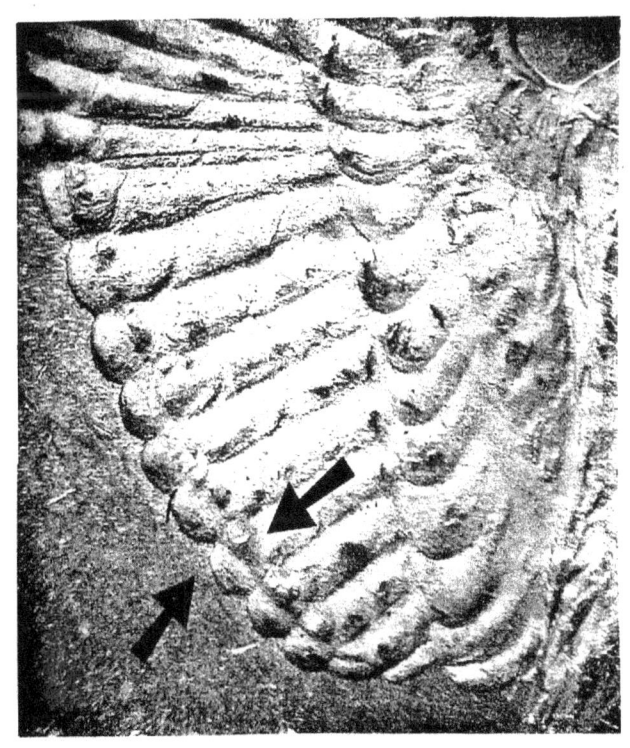

Figure 54 VAM 20 A^2/A^1/A^0 Eagle's Rt. Wing

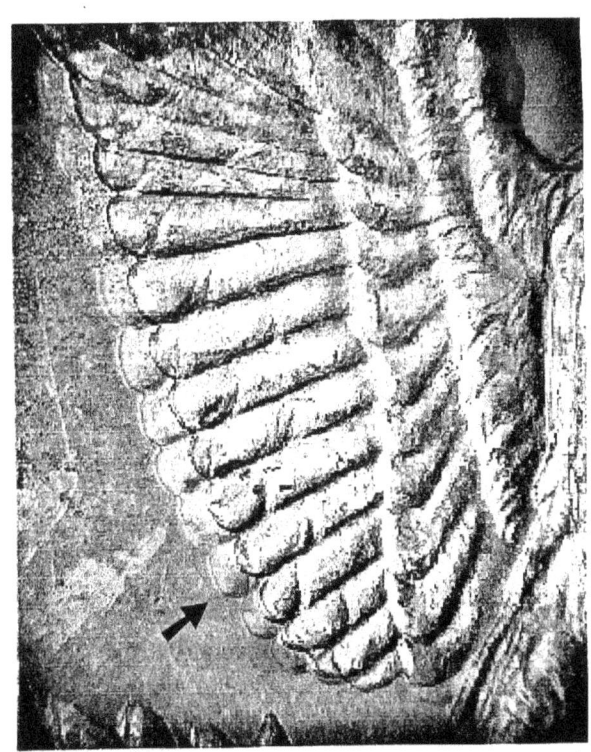

Figure 58 Photo Superposition
VAM 19 A^2 under VAM 7 A^1/A^0

Figure 57 Photo Superposition
VAM 19 A^2 over Pattern J-1550

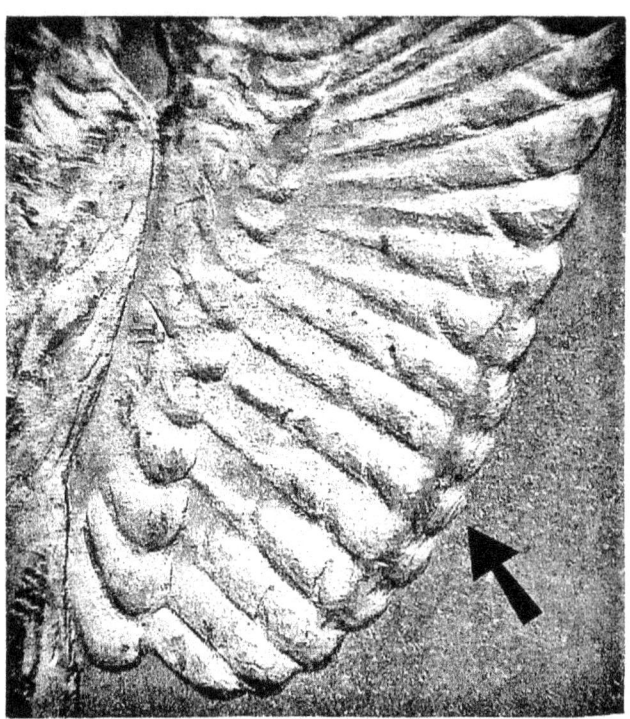

Figure 59 VAM 20 A^2/A^1/A^0 Eagle's Left Wing

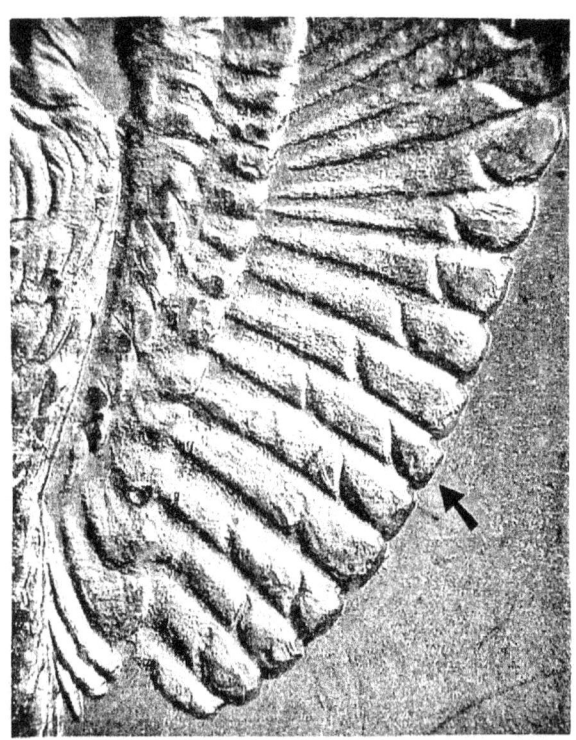

Figure 60 VAM 6 A^1/A^0 Eagle's Left Wing

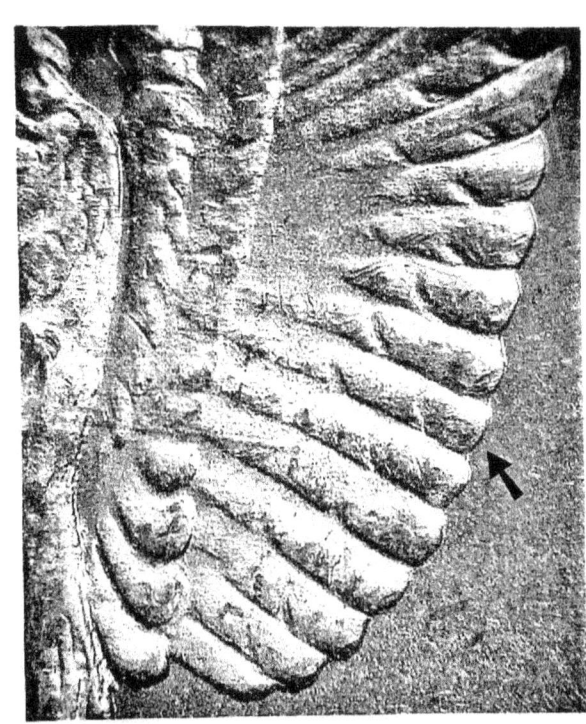

Figure 61 VAM 19 A^2 Eagle's Left Wing

Figure 62 VAM 20 Doubled Wing Top Feathers

Figure 63 VAM 19 Doubled Wing Top Feathers

Figure 64 VAM 3 I^1 Incuse M

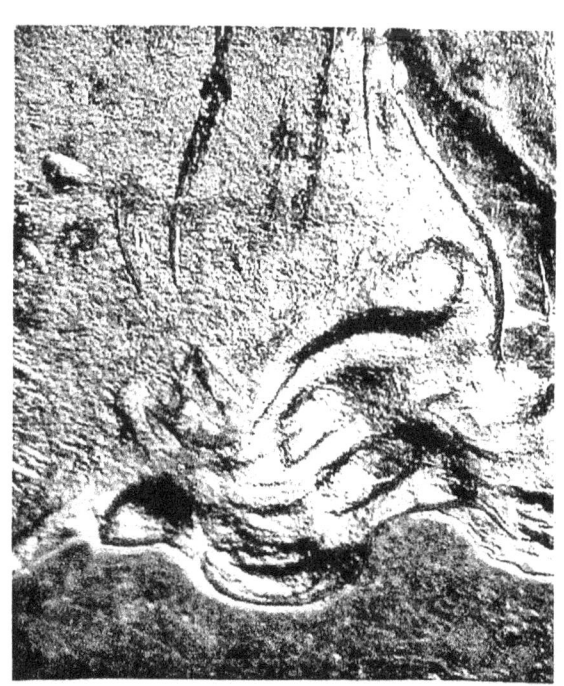

Figure 65 VAM 1 I^2 Raised M

Figure 66 VAM 16 II/I Ear

Figure 67 VAM 16 II/I LIBERTY

Figure 68 VAM 10 I Ear

Figure 69 VAM 14-1 I LIBERTY

Figure 70 VAM 195 II Ear

Figure 71 VAM 195 II LIBERTY

-30-

7 OVER 8 TAIL FEATHERS DIES

The existence of the 1878 P Morgan dollars with additional feather tips protruding between and below the ends of the 7 tail feathers variety was first reported by Samuel L. Glenhouse in a brief letter entitled, *Third Variety of 1878 Dollar?*, in the January 20, 1948 issue of *The Numismatic Scrapbook Magazine*. Subsequent articles in the same magazine included mentioning it as August 1878 7 TF ends re-engraved, by Melvin O. Carmichael in an article, *Morgan Die Varieties*, in the 1951 issue, as 1878 7 TF dies struck over 8 TF coins by Charles Wallace in an article, *Varieties of Morgan Silver Dollar*, in the February 1959 issue, and an article by Leroy Van Allen, *1878 7/8 Tail Feathers Silver Dollar: How & Why*, in the April 1965 issue which put forth the theory that eight TF dies were re-hubbed with the seven TF hub after the border lettering was lapped and polished away.

The initial 8 TF dies were unsatisfactory because they cracked and sank after a short time in the presses. Also, basining of the dies removed some of the eagle's lower wing feathers requiring each die to be touched up by an engraver to add back some feathers. The Philadelphia Mint was under pressure to meet the Bland-Allison Act minimum coinage of 2,000,000 silver dollars per month. The mint needed the new 7 TF dies with improved design relief as soon as possible to gain longer die life and to eliminate the need to touch-up each die in order to speed up coin production and to provide the San Francisco and Carson City Mints with dies so they could aid in the silver dollar production. In a letter to Superintendent Pollock on March 25, 1878 Morgan stated:

I beg to say that the new hub for reverse of silver dollar was finished and hardened today (March 25). New dies from this hub will be ready about 2nd of April but I can enter this hub into the dies- fifty in number made from the old hub and have these ready this week.

This letter indicates the possibility of a dual hub of the 8 TF reverse working dies with the new 7 TF reverse design to save a week's time in the new working die preparation. That this was carried out is indicated in Morgan's letter to Linderman on March 26:

Today I made and finished dies from the new hub for reverse of silver dollar with reference to which I reported to you yesterday. These dies are now being used in the coining room... With the dies from this hub there was no difficulty with the basins...

7 TF B Reverse Derivation

The new hub that Morgan referred to had seven tail feathers, I of In away from the eagle's wing edge, A of AMERICA touching the eagle's left wing edge, and slightly different wreaths and bow. The wreath berries have a different configuration than the A hubs and there is a noticeable wider spacing between N and E in ONE. Comparison with the B¹ reverse design shown in Figure 72 for VAM 81 with the pattern J-1550A shown in Figure 1 reveals identical motto and legend letter positions and the same wreath design. However, the lower wing feathers have been cut back and the wing widths reduced. In addition, there are nine olive leaves instead of three large ones, the rear of the arrow heads are more pointed but in the same position and the seven tail feathers are more evenly spaced with less surface detail.

Note that in the B¹ reverse of Figure 72 the notches on the feathers in the lower wings are generally two per feather and match the configuration of the feathers of the pattern J-1550A. These notches do not match the lower wing feathers of pattern J-1550 of Figure 2 or that of the A hubs designs shown previously in Figures 16 & 60 for the wings. Whereas the three A design hubs were derived from the pattern J-1550, the B design hub was derived from the pattern J-1550A.

Morgan die not have time to prepare a completely new master die. A surviving galvano of the eagle that Morgan designed and prepared for the 1877 half dollar and $10 gold patterns is shown in Figure 73. Note that the eagle is complete with arrows and olive branches with leaves that match the J-1550A pattern. To use a hub with this eagle design to make a new master die would have also required the use of a separate wreath hub to impress it's design into the master die and then the motto and legend letters would have had to be punched in by hand. As mentioned previously, Morgan had little time to prepare a new master die with eagle and wreath hubs. Besides, he had to conform to the approved design as already displayed on the struck 8 TF coins. The J-1550A pattern design was basically the same as that on the J-1550 pattern design used for the A hubs preparation. Morgan cut away the eagle's wings on a hub from the J-1550A pattern design. He also had to remove the backs of the arrow heads to make them more pointed and removed the three large olive leaves and most of the seven tail feathers. From a die made from this modified hub, he would have cut in the nine olive leaves and the slightly different 7 TF.

7/8 TF Dies Preparation

There were many design differences detailed above between the 8 TF dies made from the old hubs mentioned by Morgan and the new 7 TF B hub. The different placement of the peripheral lettering and different design wreath could have been lapped and polished away leaving most of the very similar central eagle design intact. The other possibility is that there were a number of unfinished 8 TF dies, in the middle of receiving 7 to 10 blows from the 8 TF hubs, that had only some of the central design. These unfinished 8 TF dies could have been hubbed with the 7 TF design without requiring extensive lapping and polishing. It would have saved considerable time in the working dies preparation.

Most of the 7/8 TF working dies show doubling of the central design including the eagle's wings, arrows, olive branch and leaves and sometimes the wreath bow and motto letters. The outside legend letters aren't doubled nor are most of the wreath leaves. The 8 TF A design hubs had a different legend letters location and slightly different wreath design of pattern J-1550. In order for the re-hubbed A working dies to not show doubling of the peripheral letters and wreath, each die had to have these outside areas ground and polished down before being hubbed with the different B^1 hub design. There are residual grinding and polishing marks in the motto letters and lower wreath of VAM 41 shown in Figures 74 & 75 as well as motto letters of VAM 42 shown in Figure 76.

The degree and number of tail feather ends protruding below the 7 TF design would have varied depending upon the accuracy of registration between the two designs, the amount of 8 TF design remaining when hubbed with the 7 TF design and the severity of the subsequent lapping and polishing of the dies prior to being used in the coining presses. There are currently known 13 different reverse dies of the so-called 7/8 TF variety, VAMs 30 thru 45 with the former VAM 35 eliminated and became VAM 41A with polished down die. VAMs 36 & 37 share the same reverse die with different obverse dies. These dual hub dies show varying numbers of protruding tail feathers from 3 to 7 with some doubling of the central design.

Protruding TF Ends– Pattern 7 TF or 8 TF Dies?

The strongest showing protruding tail feathers under the 7 TF of the B^1 design is that of VAM 41 die variety with 7 tips showing well below the full 7 TF as shown in Figure 77. This VAM 41 working die can be examined to determine if the Morgan dollar patterns or the A hub designs with the 8 TF match the underlying and protruding tail feather ends.

It should be noted that these protruding tail feather ends were stated to be from 7 TF patterns by Pete Bishal in the May 9, 1995 issue of *Numismatic News* and the November 20, 27 & December 4, 1995 issues of *Coin World*. He suggested that these so-called 7/8 TF die varieties be called 7/7-Pattern or 7/Pattern-7. Bishal didn't specify which of the three known Morgan dollar patterns were the underlying design nor did he show any photo overlays of the B^1 tail feathers over any pattern tail feathers.

The protruding TF ends of VAM 41 shown in Figure 77 are the most obvious differences from a normal 8 or 7 TF die. The overlying design is the B^1 reverse with 7 TF as was shown in Figure 72. A photo superposition of this B^1 7 TF reverse over the pattern J-1550A 7 TF is shown in Figure 78. The J-1550A pattern has very large and short first three tail feathers on the right as shown in Figure 1. The photo superposition shows these J-1550A right tail feathers are much shorter than the overlying B^1 tail feathers. However, the 7/8 TF die varieties of VAMs 32 & 34 thru 42 all show protruding ends below or between the 2nd & 3rd right tail feathers. (See Figure 79 of VAM 37 as an example.) Pattern J-1550A obviously couldn't be the underlying TF design. There are also major differences in the J-1550A pattern arrow heads, wing widths and olive leaves of three vs nine on the B^1 reverse that don't show up on the 7/8 TF die varieties.

The other basic pattern design is J-1550 shown in Figure 2 which had 7 TF in a configuration very close to that of the B^1 7 TF design. The J-1550 middle tail feather was a bit wider than that of the B^1 design and it had a more square end. Figure 80 shows a photo superposition of the B^1 7 TF over the J-1550 7 TF. The tail feather ends are closely lined up with each other. Both have tail feather ends that are wider than those of the 7/8 TF varieties protruding ends, particularly in the center, as shown for VAM 41 in Figure 77 and VAM 37 in Figure 79, and of other 7/8 TF die varieties shown in the VAM book. This J-1550 pattern also has a different arrow head design as well as only three large olive leaves which don't show up on the actual coins. Even if only the eagle design hub was used to re-impress the working dies, this hub still had the arrow and olive leaves on it as was previously shown in Figure 73 for the eagle galvano. The related pattern J-1552 had the same tail feathers design as J-1550 but much thinner eagle's wings, nine olive leaves that were of a slightly different configuration than the B^1 design and very pointed left ends of the arrow heads. No coins struck for circulation were exactly from either of the J-1550 or J-1552 pattern designs. However, as previously shown, the A 8 TF hubs and working dies were derived from the J-1550 pattern with many modifications.

Photo superpositions of the B^1 TF of VAM 81 over the A 8 TF of VAM 5 is shown in Figures 81 & 82. The VAM 81 7 TF is shown in Figure 83 and VAM 5 8 TF in Figure 84. Note that the protruding tail feather ends match the narrow widths of VAMs 41 & 37 protruding tail feather ends previously shown in Figures 77 & 79 and that they overlap the spaces between the B^1 7 TF on the right side as is the case for VAMs 41 & 37. No more than 7 TF ends will protrude under the B^1 TF design because the furthest right tail feather of the B^1 7 TF design (See Figure 83) is longer than that of the A 8 TF (See Figure 84). So it is obvious that the protruding tail feather ends are of an A 8 TF design. These 13 reverse die varieties are 7 over 8 tail feathers as has been commonly referred to for over 40 years.

It should be noted that some of the so-called 7/8 TF die varieties do not show protruding tail feather ends. But they show other portions of an underlying 8 TF design. VAM 30 only shows some extra talon ends shifted to the left on the olive branch and arrow shaft plus some fairly strong doubling of the middle of the inner feathers of the eagle's right wing. VAM 31 has doubled eagle's legs and other doubled features of the underlying 8 TF design. VAMs 32, 33 & 44 show 3 TF ends, VAMs 34, 36 & 37 show 4 TF ends, VAMs 38, 39 & 40 show 5 TF ends and VAMS 41 & 42 show 7 TF ends. VAM 43 shows doubled legs and other features while VAM 45 shows doubled talons and other features. Details of the 14 7/8 TF die varieties are provided in the VAM book and in the useful book by Jeff Oxman & Les Hartnett, *The 1878 Morgan Dollar 7/8-TF Attribution Guide*.

Die Doubling of Eagle's Wings

Most of the 13 so-called 7/8 TF dies have doubling of the wing feathers. VAM 42 shows doubling below the eagle's right wing lower inner wing feathers (See Figure 85). The lower underneath wider image matches the wide tip curvature of VAM 14-2 A^1/A^0 reverse (See Figure 86) while the top narrower image matches the narrow tip curvature of VAM 70 B^1 reverse (See Figure 87).

A photo superposition of the B^1 VAM 70 image of Figure 87 over the A^1/A^0 VAM 14-2 image of Figure 86 is shown in Figure 88. This photo superposition closely matches the doubling of the inner wing feathers shown previously in Figure 85 for VAM 42.

The outer feathers of the eagle's right wing also are doubled on many of the 7/8 TF dies as shown in Figure 85 for VAM 42 and Figure 89 for VAM 31. The doubling on the lower edge of the feathers continues past some of the notches as a straight line. The A reverse lower wing feathers have one notch on most of the feathers (See Figures 86 & 90 for VAM 14-2) whereas the B^1 reverse has two notches on each feather (See Figures 87 & 91). Thus, the underneath feather edges match those of the 8 TF A reverse design.

Similarly, the eagle's left wing shows doubling on the lower edge of the outer feathers of VAM 42 (See Figures 92 & 93). Again, the A design eagle's left wing feathers of VAM 4 show mostly one notch on a feather (See Figures 94 & 95) whereas the B^1 eagle's left wing feathers show two notches on each feather of VAM 81 (See Figures 96 & 97). Thus, the straight line doubling under some of the eagle's left wing feather notches in the 7/8 TF reverse is from the earlier A reverse.

VAM 31 with the strongly doubled eagle's legs also shows doubled lower inner feathers of the eagle's right wing and the outer feathers of the eagle's right wing that show doubled lines below the notches of the B^1 over A design (See Figure 98). There are also feather tips at the junctions of the feathers near the edge of the eagle's right wing that are the shorter feather ends of the underlying A design (See Figure 99). VAM 41 shows similar underlying feather ends of the narrow A wing along the edge of the eagle's right wing as shown in Figure 100. A photo superposition of B^1 eagle's lower right wing of VAM 81 of Figure 101 over the A^1/A^0 lower wing of VAM 14-3 in Figure 16 is shown in Figure 102 which indicates a wider wing of the B^1 design. The narrower A^1/A^0 wing width shows and closely resembles the length of the feather tips on the edges of VAMs 31 & 41 shown previously. A whole coin photo superposition of the B^1 VAM 81 design of Figure 72 over the A^1/A^0 design of VAM 14-3 of Figure 5 is shown in Figure 103. The wider eagle's wings of the B^1 design is apparent as is the mis-matched legend letters.

The feather tips at the edge of VAMs 31 & 41 eagle's right wing aren't an underlying J-1550A pattern as the pattern wings are obviously much wider and extend further down to the leg as was shown in Figure 1. The J-1550 eagle's right wing lower portion is also wider than the B^1 design as shown in the photo superposition of VAM 81 over J-1550 of Figure 104.

There is also doubling at the top of the eagle's right wing on VAMs 32, 34 & 42 as shown in Figures 105, 106 & 107. At the right side of the first tier of circular feather ends, the doubling goes under some of the notches indicating a B^1 over A design as was shown lower down on the eagle's right and left wing feathers. But the **key item** is some feather ends below the second and third feathers from the bottom that are set well to the right of the visible feather tier ends. These are remnants of the **jagged tier feather ends** found **only** on the A design as previously shown in Figures 21-25 and 62 & 63. The three Morgan reverse patterns show a circular upper tier feather ends as does the B^1 reverse shown in Figure 108. So the 7/8 TF die varieties are definitely A working dies hubbed over with the B^1 design.

Note that the top two feathers just to the left of this first tier of feather ends are narrow for the A^1/A^0 designs (See Figures 21-25), the 7/8 TF (See Figures 105, 106 & 107) and the B^1 design (See Figure 108). These two feathers are wider on the $A^2/A^1/A^0$ design shown in Figures 62 & 63 for VAMs 20 & 19. The doubling of the 7/8 TF varieties don't show any trace of these wider $A^2/A^1/A^0$ top two feathers. This may be due to this area being polished off on the re-hubbed working dies.

There is a raised large circular dot on top of the lower-most inner feather of the eagle's left wing on VAMs 33 & 45 shown in Figures 109 & 110. VAM 42 also shows part of this circular dot as was shown in Figure 93. This is from the high relief lower-most inner feather of the A^2 reverse design of VAM 19. See Figure 111 which shows a smaller feather than that of the B^1 reverse of VAM 81shown in Figure 97. These three 7/8 TF dies of VAMs 33, 42 & 45 show definite evidence of the A^2 hub design on top of the B^1 inner feather design.

Die Doubling on Legs, Olive Leaves, Arrow Heads and Wreath Bow

Moving down to the eagle's legs, there are four bands on the eagle's bare left legs for all three A 8 TF and the B^1 reverse designs (See Figures 40, 41, 42 & 112). But there are only two bands on the eagle's wider right leg on the A^1/A^0 and A^2 reverses (See Figures 113 & 114). This was changed to four bands on the eagle's thinner right leg for the B^1 reverse to match the eagle's left leg (See Figure 115). The so-called 7/8 TF reverse shows various degrees of the two to four bands on the eagle's bare right leg. For example, VAM 32 shows a wide eagle's right leg with two bands on the right side and four on the left side of this leg (See Figure 116). VAM 40 shows a wide leg of two bands with the different band angles merging in the leg center (See Figure 117). Note that the A^1/A^0 top band of the eagle's right leg has a raised dot in the middle (See Figure 113) whereas the A^2 top band does not (See Figure 114). The fewer bands on the eagle's right leg indicate remnants of an A design but there aren't enough of the A wide bands showing to determine if the dot on the top band of A^1/A^0 is there.

There are differences in the olives on the olive branch among the A^1/A^0, A^2 & B^1 designs as shown in Figures 118, 119 & 120. The A^1/A^0 olive used on VAMs 1-17 has a large olive on top with a large raised portion below the olive branch with blunt left end. The $A^2/A^1/A^0$ olive used on VAMs 18-23 have a small olive and small oblong raised portion below the olive branch that blends into the branch on both sides. The B^1 olive is large and set further left of the eagle's talon with no portions below the olive branch.

Figure 121 shows the remnants of the underlying olive and olive branch below the full B^1 olive and olive branch of VAM 32. The remnant raised portion below the remnant olive branch is cut off on the left side matching the A^1/A^0 raised portion shown in Figure 118. Thus, the VAM 32 was an A^1/A^0 working die re-hubbed with the B^1 hub. It also has strong doubling of the top feathers of the eagle's right wing (See Figure 105) characteristic of A^1/A^0 dies. VAM 34 shows in Figure 122 a similar remnant of the raised portion of the olive and doubling at the top of the eagle's right wing of A^1/A^0 design (See Figure 106). VAM 38 is similar with A^1/A^0 remnant olive (See Figure 123) but has only slight doubling at the top of the eagle's right wing.

VAMs 33, 40 & 42 show a remnant of the olive lower portion (See Figures 124, 125 & 126) that matches the A^2 olive without any doubling at the top of the eagle's right wing. So these working dies were of the $A^2/A^1/A^0$ design re-hubbed with the B^1 hub design. Some of the other 7/8 TF working dies show remnants of an olive and branch, such as VAMs 37, 39 & 41, but are too faint to determine the type of olive. But it can be concluded from the olive remnants previously shown that **both the A^1/A^0 and $A^2/A^1/A^0$ working dies** were re-hubbed with the B^1 hub design.

Neither patterns J-1550 nor J-1550A had an olive on the olive branch as shown in Figures 1 & 2. Pattern J-1552 shown in Figure 3 has a very small olive on top of the olive branch and a large raised portion below the branch. Other design differences in the pattern J-1552, such as in the olive leaves and arrow heads plus the much narrower eagle's wings and 7 TF also eliminate this design as an underlying one of the 7/8 TF die varieties. Besides, there is no evidence of working dies or coins struck from this pattern design.

It should be noted that VAM 41 shows an underlying vertical olive leaf to the right of the top rightmost olive leaf of the A design as is shown in Figure 127. The B^1 top rightmost leaf has a curve on the right outside as does the A^2 olive leaf shown in Figure 128. The straight side of this rightmost olive leaf for the A^1/A^0 design was previously shown in Figures 29-33 and it is closer to the olive. Thus, VAM 41 shows an underlying rightmost top olive leaf of the A^1/A^0 design. VAM 37 shows a similar underlying olive leaf.

Next, consider the arrow heads of VAM 42 (See Figure 129). It shows the remains of another arrow head below the middle arrow head. The left end of the underneath arrow head is in the same position as the left end of the A^2 middle arrow head of VAM 22 (See Figure 43) which is in the same position for the A^1/A^0 arrow head of VAM 17 (See Figure 34). The B^1 middle arrow head is further to the left with the rear edge even with the center of the upper and lower arrow heads (See Figure 130). There is not any underlying remains above the top arrow head and shaft for VAM 42 of Figure 129 that would likely be there for the A^1/A^0 slanted upwards top arrow head and shaft (See Figure 34). So the underlying remains is $A^2/A^1/A^0$. The left back edge of Judd Pattern J-1550 & J-1550A middle arrow head is nearly even with the left edges of the upper and lower arrow heads. The J-1552 pattern back edge is a little further left than A^2. (See Figures 1, 2 & 3) The pattern middle arrow heads don't match this remnant on VAM 42.

The wreath bow of VAM 42 shows doubling on the lower left and right sides (See Figure 131) and VAM 37 shows doubling on the lower right side (See Figure 132) that are remnants of the A bow. The wreath bow width was wider for the A^2 reverse (See Figure 47) than that for the B^1 reverse (See Figure 133). VAM 42 also shows an extra berry in the left wreath opposite the lower olive leaf ends (See Figure 134). This is the remains of the high relief berry o the A left wreath (See Figure 135).

As a final note, VAM 30 with doubled talons shows very little of any underlying remnants or doubling of the A design. There are extra talons to the left of both left and right legs middle talons. There is also some widely spaced doubling of the middle inner feathers of the eagle's right wing shown in Figure 136. These have a rounded left edge of the A design shown in Figures 12, 15 & 16 rather than the more squared off left edge of the B^1 design (See Figure 101).

7/8 TF Die Doubling Conclusions

The 13 working dies with various numbers of protruding tail feather ends are the 7 TF B^1 reverse design hubbed over the 8 TF A reverse working dies, **as has been so obvious for the past 40 years**. The underlying protruding tail feather tips match those of the 8 TF A reverse, using photo superpositions, in feather width and placement. They do not match any of the three Morgan patterns tail feathers. The patterns all had 7 TF with cut-back right tail feathers on pattern J-1550A or wide middle feathers on patterns J-1550 and J-1552 that don't match the protruding feather tips in width or lateral placement on the various 7/8 TF working dies. These 13 working dies should still be called 7/8 TF die varieties.

Die doubling of the 7/8 TF working dies on the lower inner feathers of the eagle's right wing match the photo superposition of the B^1 7 TF design over the A^1/A^0 8 TF design.

Die doubling of the 7/8 TF working dies outer wing feathers of both wings shows underlying feather edges that go under the additional feather notches of the B^1 design. The A design wing feathers have fewer feather notches than the B^1 design. The A design is the underlying feather edges of the doubled B^1 wing feathers.

Both VAMs 31 & 41 show feather tip die doubling near the outside edge of the eagle's right wing. A photo superposition shows that the tips of the narrower A wing are at this same position as the underlying doubling of wider B^1 wings.

There are remnants of the **jagged** tier of feather ends found only on the A design at the top of the eagle's right wing on VAMs 32, 34 & 42. All three patterns have a **circular** upper tier of feather ends and **could not** have caused these feather tip remnants.

The eagle's right legs show remnants of the A two bands on the 7/8 TF working dies whereas the B^1 design had four bands.

Some 7/8 TF working dies show remnants of the A^1/A^0 olive or the different A^2 olive below the olive branch. The B^1 olive had a different design that was only on top of the olive branch. Patterns J-1550 and J-1550A didn't have an olive and the one on the J-1552 pattern was of a different design. This is **positive proof** that **both** the A^1/A^0 and $A^2/A^1/A^0$ working dies were re-hubbed with the B^1 hub design.

Both VAMS 37 & 41 show a remnant right-most top olive leaf that matches the A^1/A^0 straight right edge and not the curved edge of the A^2 or B^1 designs.

VAM 42 shows a remnant arrow head edge below the middle arrow head that matches the position of the A middle arrow head and **not** the three patterns.

VAMs 37 & 42 show remnants of the wider A wreath bow to the sides of the narrower B^1 bow. VAM 42 also shows an extra berry remnant in the left wreath opposite the lower olive leaf ends that matches the A wreath berry position.

The 7/8 TF die varieties are thus A^1/A^0 and $A^2/A^1/A^0$ working dies that were re-hubbed with the B^1 design. The underlying protruding tail feather tips and the various doubling **are of A designs** and **not** of any of the three Morgan pattern designs. These 13 die varieties should still be called **7/8 Tail Feathers** as they have been for the past 40 years. They are **more** than just simple die doubling of one hub design shifting between hub blows that would produce a shadow outline type of doubling on the tail feather ends (Such as the 1901 P VAM 3 Shifted Eagle). Technically, they are $B^1/A^1/A^0$ and $B^1/A^2/A^{1'}/A^0$ triple and quadrupled hubs of **differing** designs.

7/8 TF Reverse and Obverse Die Combinations/Sequences

The 13 7/8 TF reverse dies combined with obverse dies are given below. These multiple hub reverse dies were paired with the dual hub obverse II/I die varieties and the II obverse design type. The II/I obverse ear has a short pointed inner ear fill with equally divided right side of ear (See Figure 66). The II obverse ear has a long blunted inner ear fill and unequally divided right side of the ear (See Figure 70). Further design details are given in the VAM book.

B/Aa– II/I 7 (VAM 30)
B/Ab– II/I 8 (VAM 31)
B/Ac– II 2 (VAM 32)
B/Ad– II/I 7 (VAM 33), II/I 37 (VAM 44)   B/Ad die sequence: 44, 33
B/Ae– II 2 (VAM 34)
B/Af– (Eliminated, polished down B/Ak)

B/Ag– II 1 (VAM 36), II 2 (VAM 37) B/Af die sequence: 36, 37
B/Ah– II/I 9 (VAM 38)
B/Ai– II 2 (VAM 39)
B/Aj– II/I 8 (VAM 40)
B/Ak– II 2 (VAM 41)
B/Al– II/I 5 (VAM 42)
B/Am– II/I 3 (VAM 43)
B/An– II 2 (VAM 45)

Possible obverse die sequences:
    II/I 5:   17, 42
    II/I 7:   81, 33, 30 (Die crack 187)
    II/I 8:   40, 31, 110 (Die crack neck to first left star)

SUMMARY

First 8 Tail Feather Designs–
- Listed in VAM book as A^1 reverse design. Fourteen working reverse dies were used.
- These dies show extensive but different die doubling of hub misalignment, dual hub designs, radial direction size differences and design differences remnants.
- Each die had lower wing feathers engraved back into the working die when the original feathers were unintentionally removed by the die polishing process.
- Die doubling shows **two slightly different design** 8 TF hubs, A^0 & A^1, were used to make the working dies.
- None of the three Morgan dollar pattern hubs were used to make the working dies since they all had major design differences (different size eagle's wings and 7 TF) and these differences didn't show up on the coins. A^0 and A^1 designs were **derived from the J-1550 pattern design.**
- Minor design differences in the two 8 TF hubs, A^0 and A^1, were in one olive leaf and the eagle's top and lower wing feathers which caused die doubling of these areas.
- Doubling of the wreath leaves and legend letters was caused by slightly different diameter of the outer design of the two 8 TF hubs from incorrect hardening or annealing process.
- Initial 8 TF reverse identification in the VAM book as only A^1 should now be designated as A^1/A^0. Neither the A^0 nor A^1 design has been seen alone on a working die.

Second 8 TF "Dual" Hub Combination–
- Designated as A^2/A^1 dual hub in VAM book and characterized by doubled eagle's beak and I of In is away from eagle's wing. Five working dies were used.
- Engraver George Morgan created a third version of the 8 TF design, A^2, with **small** design changes that showed up on the coins as die doubling or design differences with the underlying doubling **matching** the A^1/A^0 design.
- None of the three pattern hubs were used to modify these 8 TF working dies since there were significant design differences that didn't show up on the coins.
- Changes made in the A^2 design were made to correct difficulties experienced with the A^1/A^0 design working dies that had parts of the lower wing feathers removed when the working dies were polished and in low die lifetimes.
- To make these small design changes, Morgan removed details by cutting them away on a hub or strengthened details by cutting them into a die.
- Changes on the A^2 design from the A^1/A^0 design that caused doubling of working die areas include a sharper hook on the eagle's beak, bottom edge of eagle's right wing had one feather added and bottom edge of left wing had two feathers enlarged and one removed, top arrow head and shaft was moved down, wreath bow was strengthened on left side, wreath leaf next to upper left of bow was cut back, top left leaf of second from top leaf cluster of left wreath was eliminated and a berry and vertical branch put in it's place, and eagle's right wing was widened.
- A^2 design is a **derivative** of previously used A^1/A^0 designs but was **never used alone**; only as hub over A^1/A^0 working dies.
- A^2/A^1 "dual" hub five reverse die varieties listed in the VAM book are actually a triple hub, designated as

$A^2/A^1/A^0$, for this second 8 TF design series working dies.

7 Over 8 Tail Feathers Dies–

● Listed in VAM book as 7/8 TF reverse die varieties and they are characterized by various numbers of tail feather ends protruding below 7 tail feathers design. 13 different reverse dies are known.

● Each working die shows different degrees of doubling and protruding tail feather ends. The overlapping design is **B^1 derived from pattern J-1550A.**

● The protruding tail feather tips **match** those of the **8 TF A reverse design** using photo superpositions. The protruding tips do **not** match any of the three Morgan dollar pattern 7 TF tips width or position.

● Differences in 7 TF & 8 TF designs showed up on coins as doubling of eagle's right wing inner feathers, outer feathers of left and right wings, top feathers of eagle's right wing, eagle's bare right leg, middle arrow head, olive and top rightmost olive leaf, left and right outside of wreath bow, and some wreath berries and leaves.

● Die doubling of the lower inner feathers of eagle's right wing and outer feathers of both wings matches photo super position of B^1 design over A design.

● Photo superposition of wider B^1 eagle's wings over narrower A wings matches eagle's right wing edge doubling of VAMs 31 & 41.

● Top of eagle's right wing of VAMs 32, 34 & 42 show remnants of **jagged tier** of feather ends **unique** to A design and **not** found on **circular tier** of all three Morgan dollar patterns.

● Eagle's right leg shows remnants of A two bands vs four bands of B^1 design.

● There are remnants of **unique A^1/A^0 olive** and different $A^2/A^1/A^0$ **olive** below olive branch on many 7/8 TF working dies. Patterns J-1550 and J-1550A didn't have an olive and pattern J-1552 had a different olive design.

● VAMs 37 & 41 show remnant of rightmost top olive leaf that matches A^1/A^0 straight right edge and not the curved A^2 or B^1 designs.

● Remnant of arrow head edge below middle arrow head on VAM 42 **matches A design position** and not any of the three pattern middle arrow heads.

● Remnants of wider wreath bow of A design show on VAMs 37 & 42 bows as well as a remnant A design extra berry in lower left wreath on VAM 42 die.

● **None** of the three dollar Morgan pattern hub designs match the underlying images of the doubled areas. Top design image matches the B^1 7 TF design used in regular coinage.

● B^1 design was hubbed into A design working dies that were only partially hubbed with **incomplete** designs, or the outer lettering and wreath had been **lapped and polished** away so differences in the B^1 & A designs in these areas would not cause major die doubling.

● These dual hub working dies should still be called **7/8 TF die varieties** because the underneath tail feathers were from 8 TF working dies and **not** the Morgan dollar 7 TF pattern designs. They are not a simple shadow outline type of doubling from a hub misalignment between hub blows. (Such as for 1901 P VAM 3 Shifted Eagle.)

● These triple and quadrupled hubs are 7 TF B^1 design hub over 8 TF $A^2/A^1/A^0$ and A^1/A^0 designs working dies, designated as $B^1/A^1/A^0$ and $B^1/A^2/A^1/A^0$.

Figure 72 VAM 81 B¹ Reverse

Figure 73 Morgan Eagle Galvano
Photo courtesy Coinage 1984

Figure 74 VAM 41 File Lines in Motto

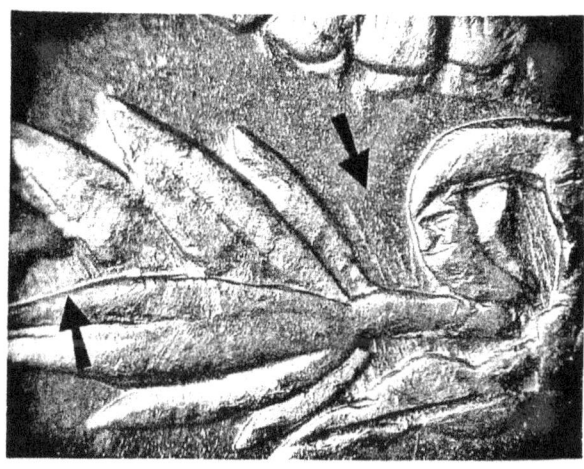

Figure 75 VAM 41 File Lines in Wreath

Figure 76 VAM 42 File Lines in Motto

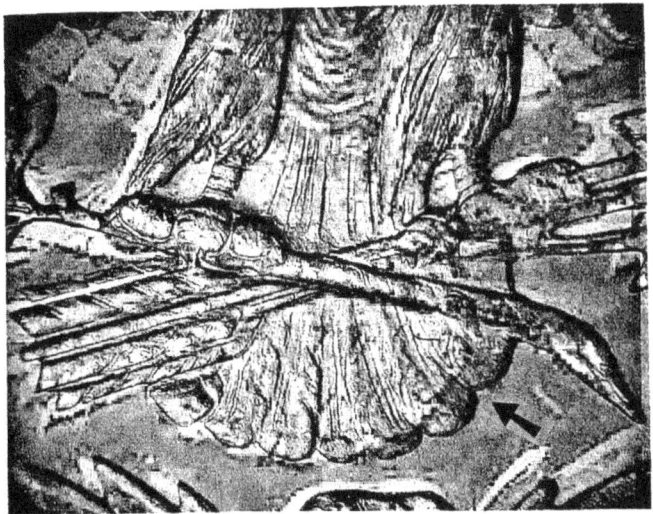

Figure 78 Photo Superposition
VAM 81 B^1 over Pattern J-1550A

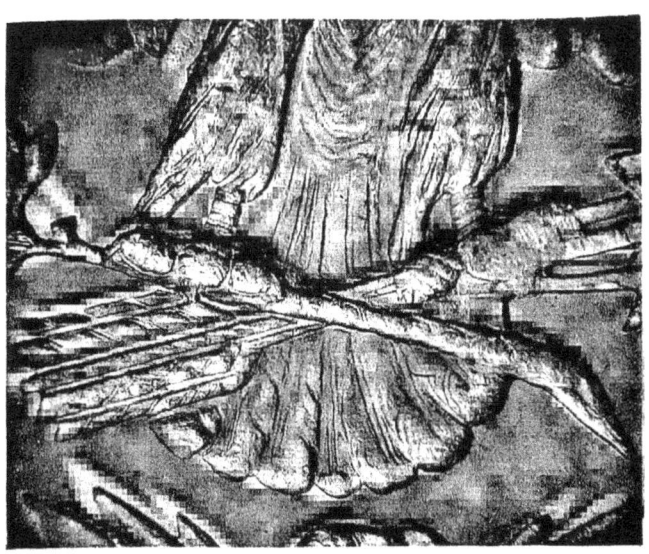

Figure 80 Photo Superposition
VAM 81 B^1 over Pattern J-1550

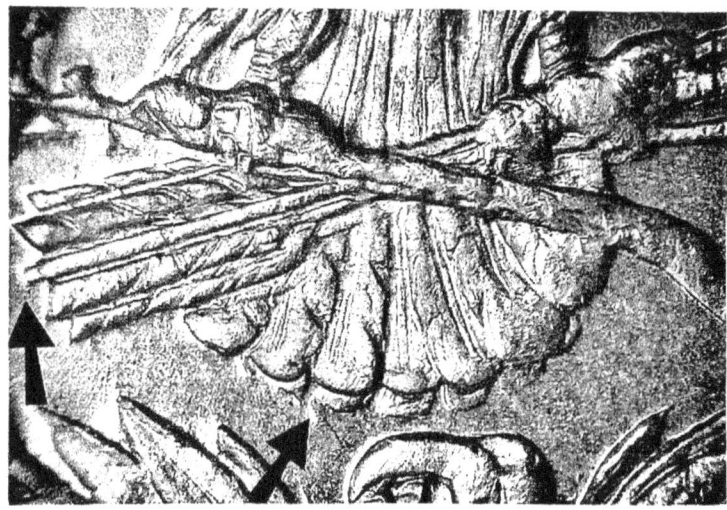

Figure 77 VAM 41 7/8 Tail Feathers

Figure 79 VAM 37 7/8 Tail Feathers

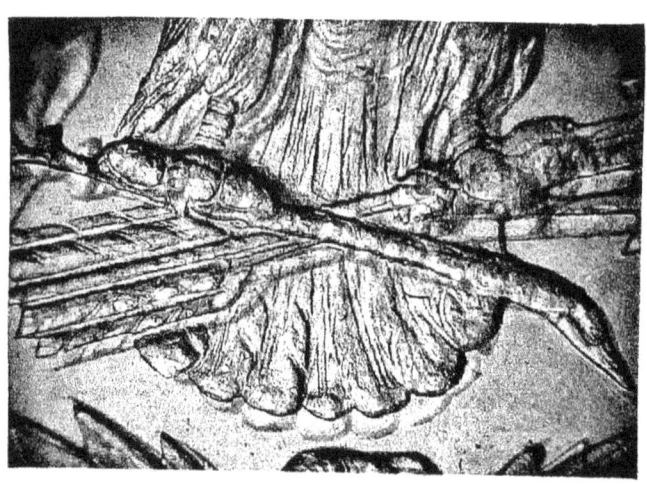

Figure 81 Photo Superposition
VAM 81 B^1 7 TF over VAM 5 A 8 TF

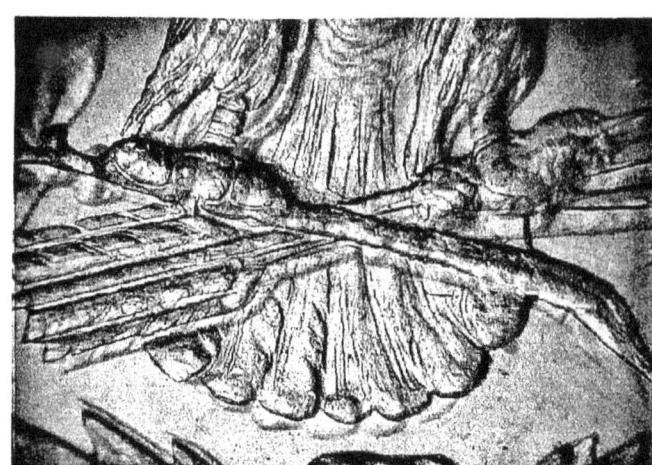

Figure 82 Photo Superposition
VAM 81 B^1 7 TF over VAM 5 A 8 TF

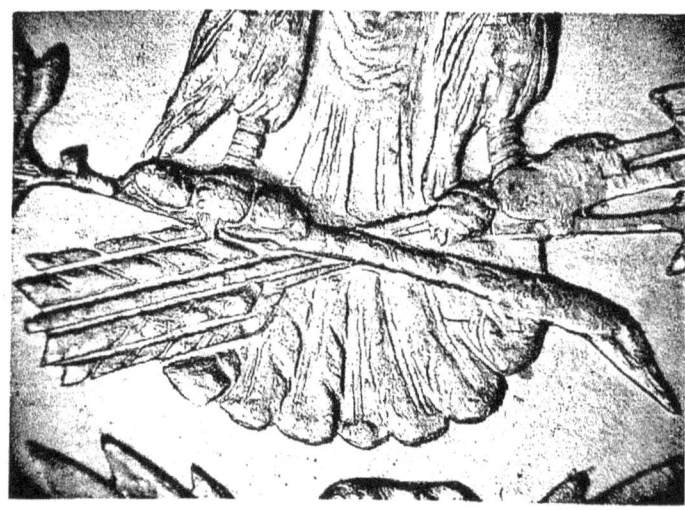

Figure 83 VAM 81 B^1 7 Tail Feathers

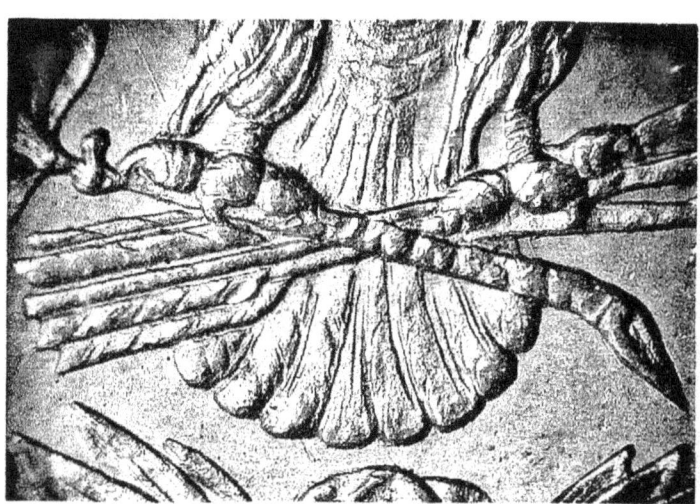

Figure 84 VAM 5 A 8 Tail Feathers

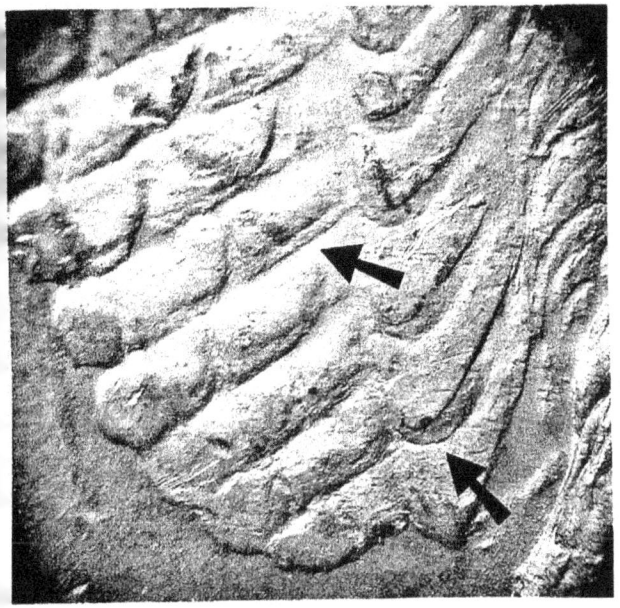

Figure 85 VAM 42 Doubled Lower Feathers

Figure 86 VAM 14-2 A^1/A^0 Lower Feathers

Figure 87 VAM 70 B^1 Lower Feathers

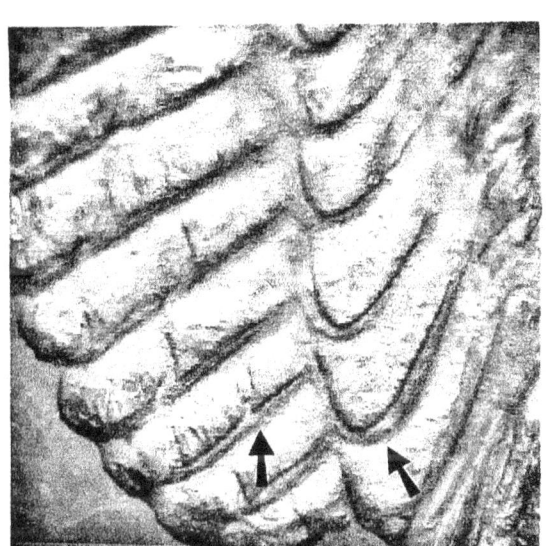

Figure 88 Photo Superposition
VAM 70 B^1 over VAM 14-2 A^1/A^0

Figure 89 VAM 31 B^1/A Doubled Middle Feathers

Figure 90 VAM 14-2 Middle Feathers

Figure 91 VAM 83 B^1 Middle Feathers

Figure 92 VAM 42 Doubled Middle Feathers

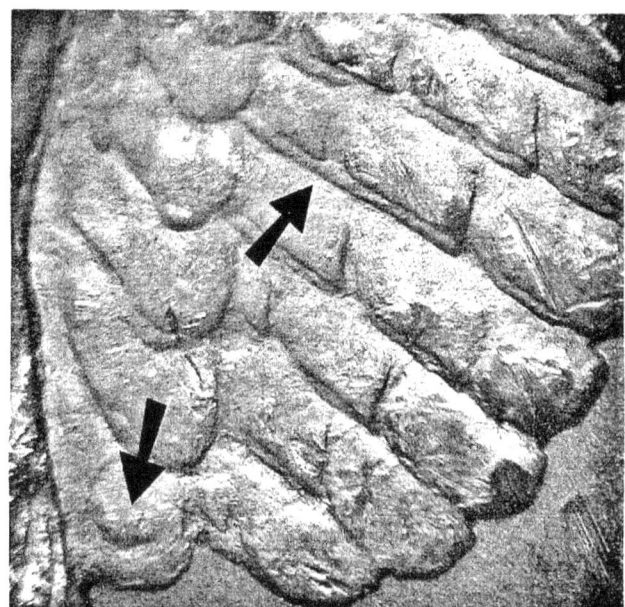

Figure 93 VAM 42 Doubled Lower Feathers

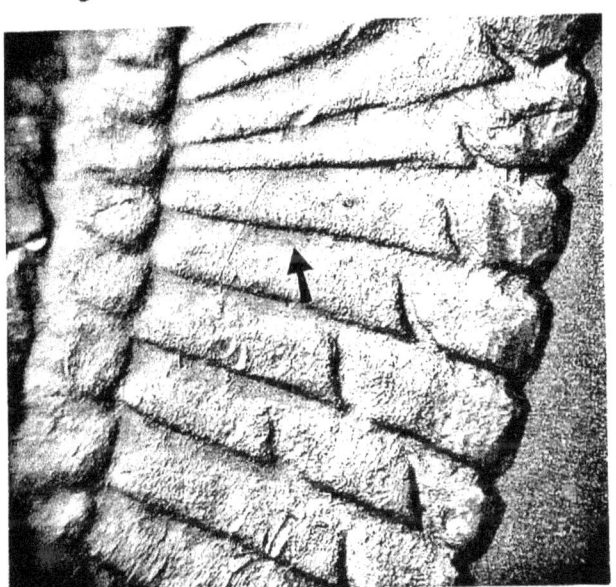

Figure 94 VAM 4 A¹/A⁰ Middle Feathers

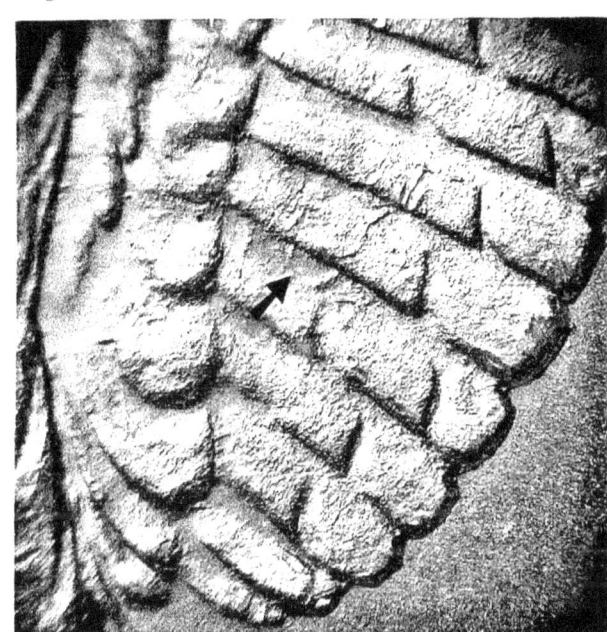

Figure 95 VAM 4 A¹/A⁰ Lower Feathers

Figure 96 VAM 81 B¹ Middle Feathers

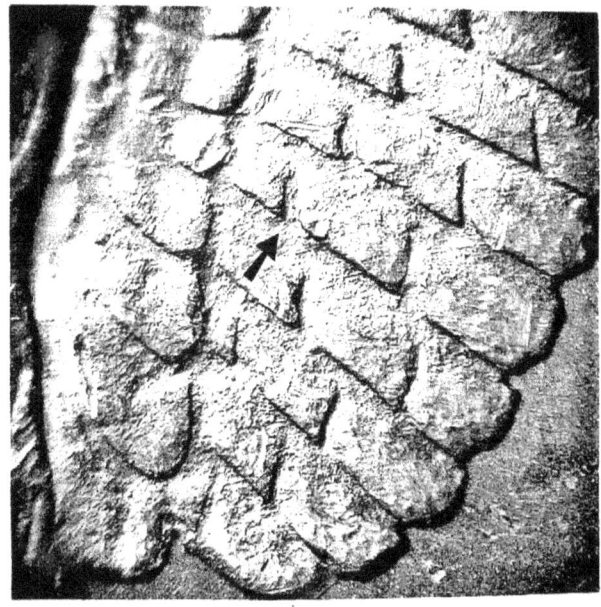

Figure 97 VAM 81 B¹ Lower Feathers

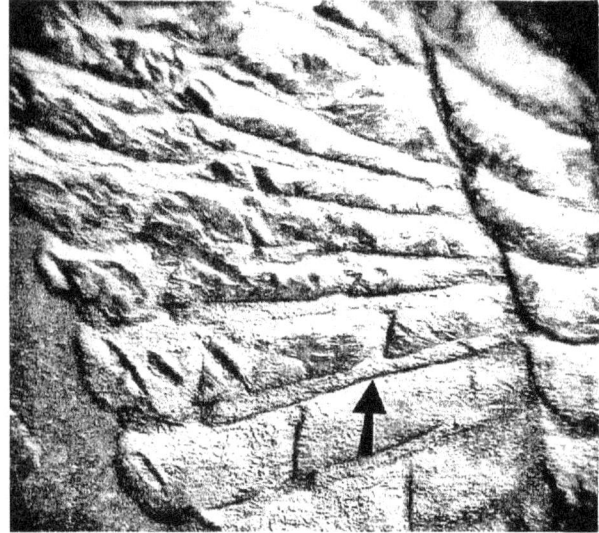

Figure 98 VAM 31 Doubled Middle Feathers

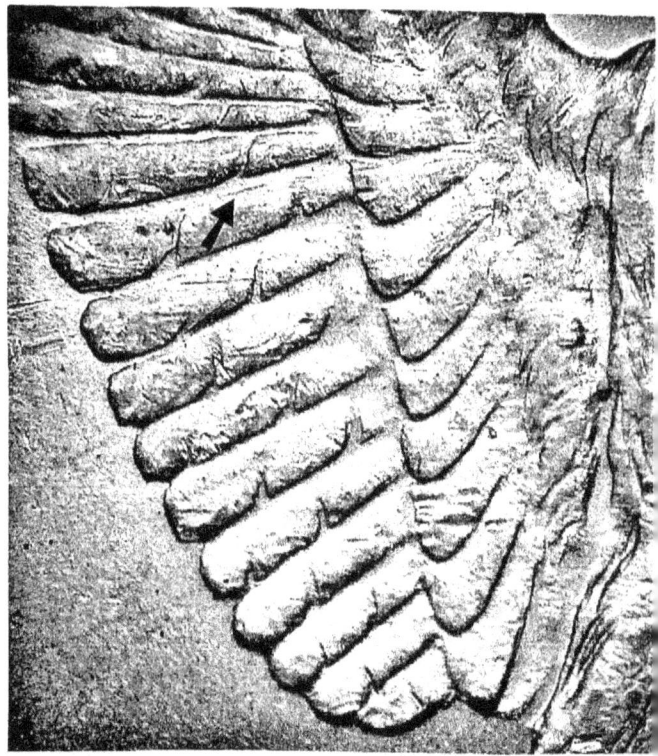

Figure 99 VAM 31 Lower Doubled Feathers

Figure 100 VAM 41 Doubled Lower Feathers

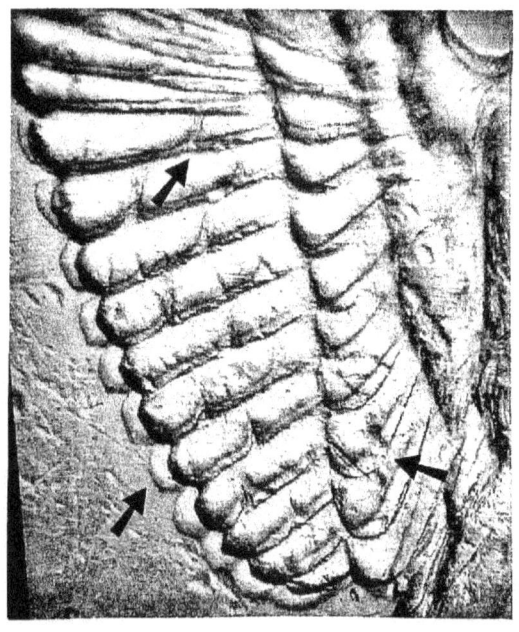

Figure 101 VAM 81 B^1 Lower Feathers

Figure 102 Photo Superposition
VAM 14-3 A^1/A^0 over VAM 81 B^1

-44-

Figure 103 Photo Superposition
VAM 81 B^1 over VAM 14-3 A^1/A^0

Figure 104 Photo Superposition
VAM 81 B¹ over Pattern J-1550

Figure 105 VAM 32 Doubled Feathers

Figure 106 VAM 34 Doubled Feathers

Figure 107 VAM 42 Doubled Feathers

Figure 108 VAM 81 B¹ Top of Wing

Figure 109 VAM 33 A^2 Raised Dot

Figure 110 VAM 45 A^2 Raised Dot

Figure 111 VAM 19 A^2 Lower Feathers

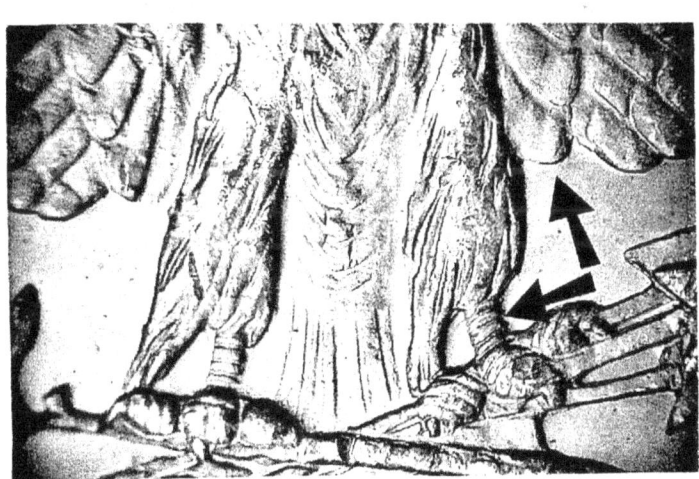

Figure 112 VAM 83 B^1 Bottom of Wings

Figure 113 VAM 9 A^1/A^0 Eagle's Rt. Leg

Figure 114 VAM 19 A^2 Eagle's Rt. Leg

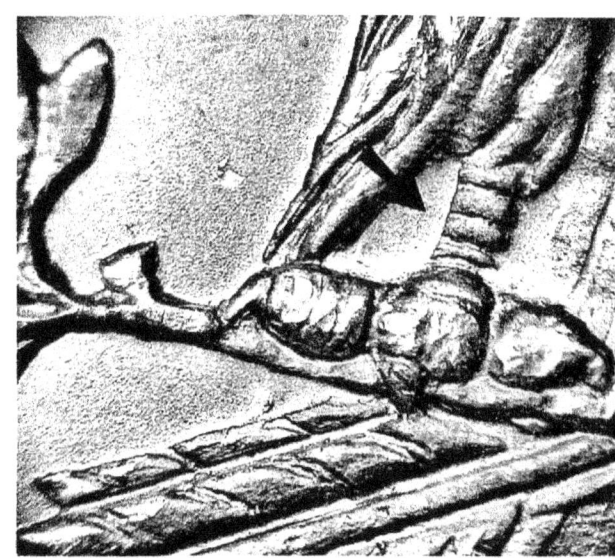

Figure 115 VAM 83 B^1 Eagle's Rt. Leg

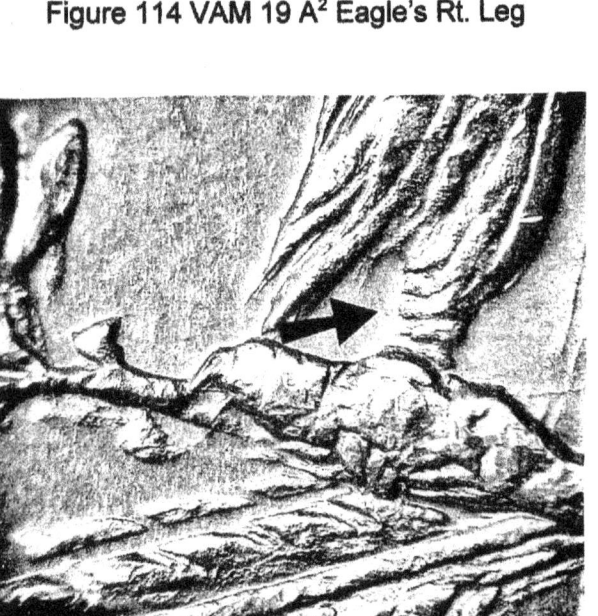

Figure 116 VAM 32 B^1/A^2 Eagle's Rt. Leg

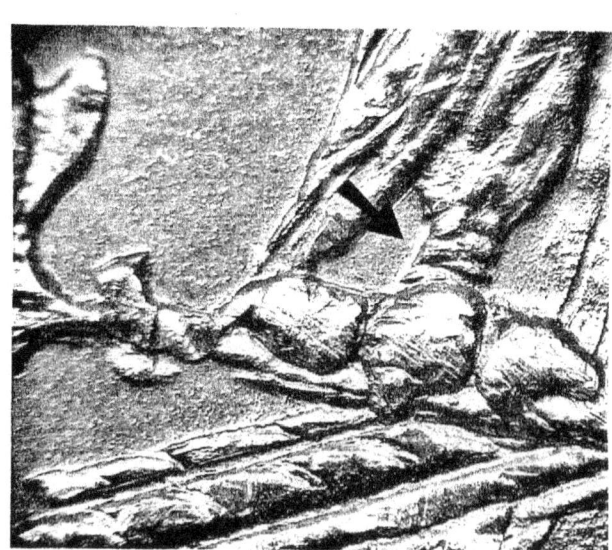

Figure 117 VAM 40 B^1/A^2 Eagle's Rt. Leg

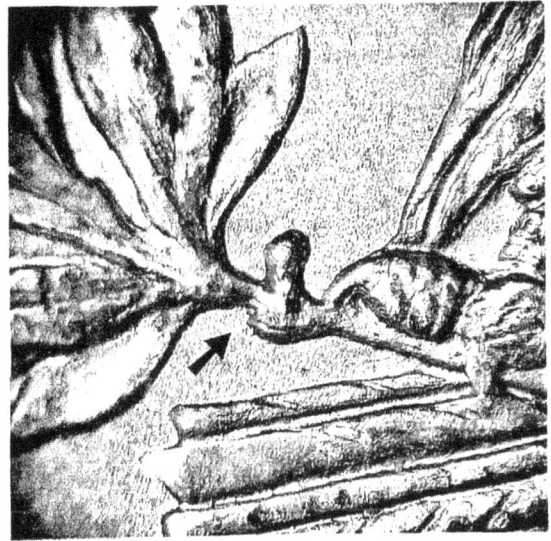

Figure 118 VAM 14-2 A¹/A⁰ Olive

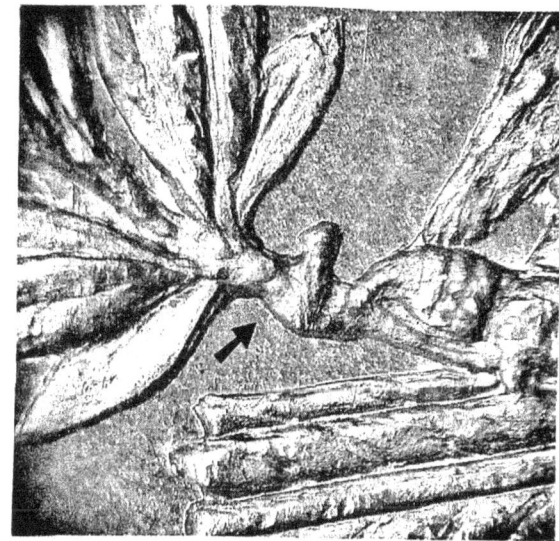

Figure 119 VAM 20 A² Olive

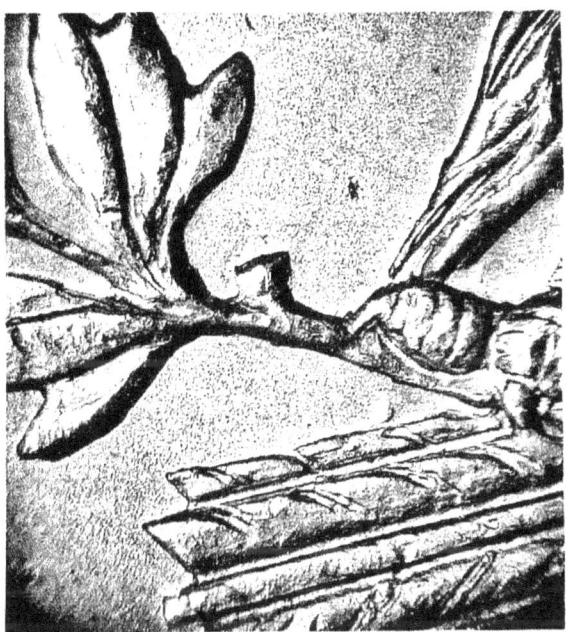

Figure 120 VAM 83 B¹ Olive

Figure 121 VAM 32 Remnant Olive

Figure 122 VAM 34 Remnant Olive

Figure 123 VAM 38 Remnant Olive

Figure 124 VAM 33 Remnant Olive

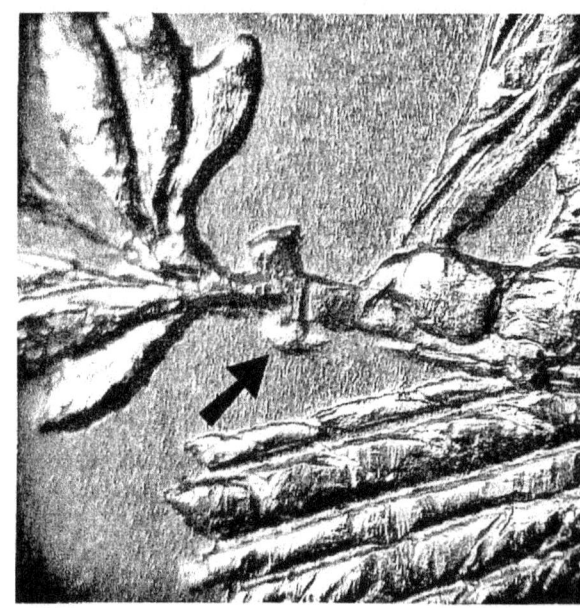

Figure 125 VAM 40 Remnant Olive

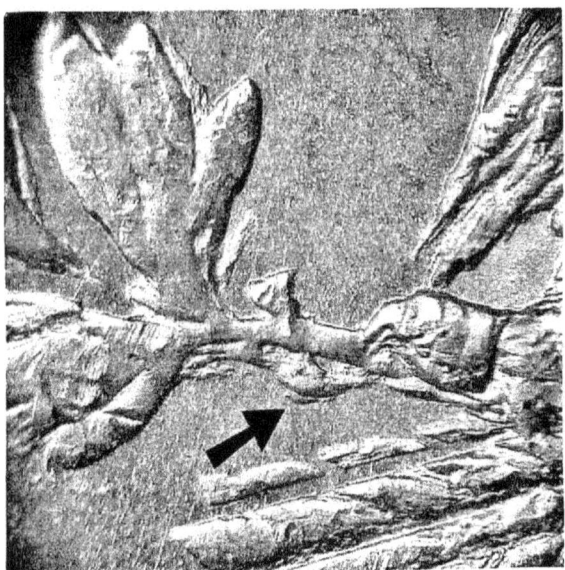

Figure 126 VAM 42 Remnant Olive

Figure 127 VAM 41 B^1/A^1/A^0 Olive Leaves

Figure 128 VAM 19 A^2 Olive Leaves

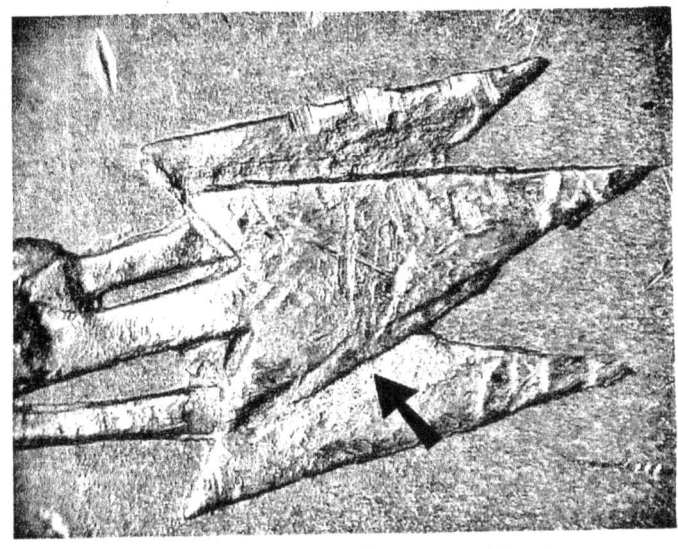

Figure 129 VAM 42 B^1/A Arrow Heads

Figure 130 VAM 83 B^1 Arrow Heads

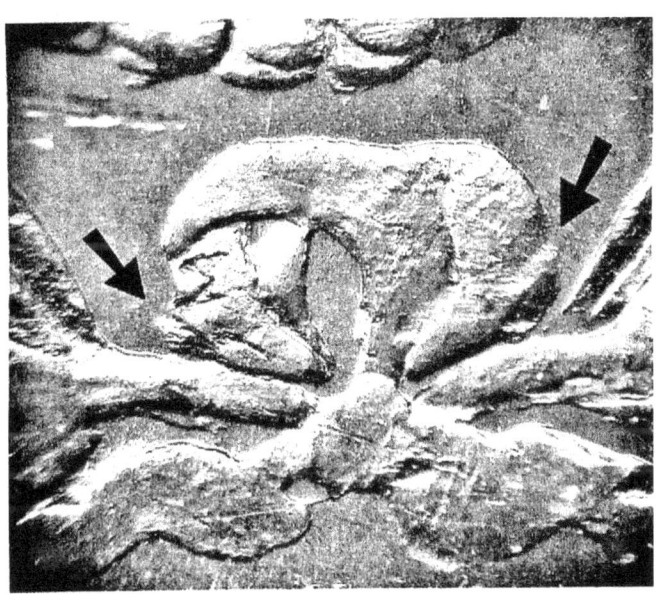

Figure 131 VAM 42 B^1/A Doubled Wreath Bow

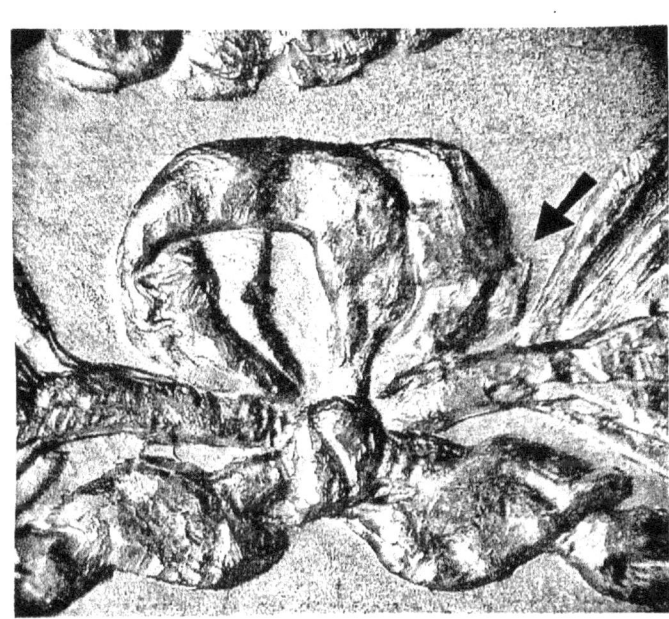

Figure 132 VAM 37 B^1/A Doubled Wreath Bow

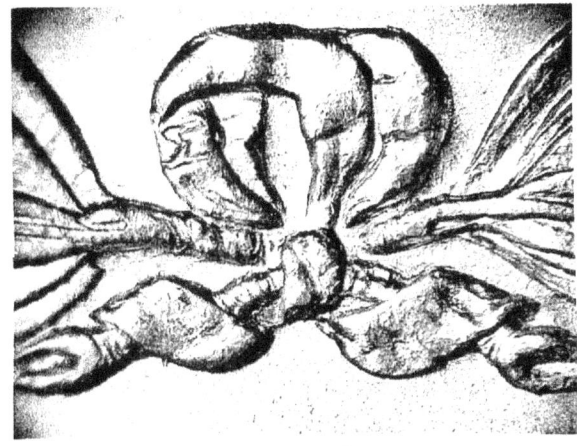

Figure 133 VAM 83 B^1 Wreath Bow

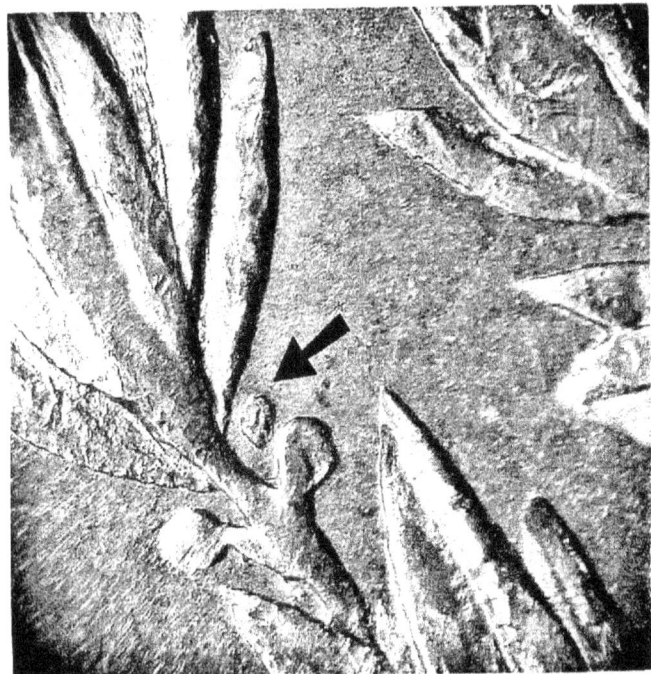

Figure 134 VAM 42 B^1/A Extra Berry Left Wreath

Figure 135 VAM 19 A Middle Left Wreath

Figure 136 VAM 30 Doubled Inner Feathers

FURTHER REFERENCES

Please check Amazon Kindle for Michael S. Fey, Ph.D., and Leroy Van Allen & A. George Mallis publications. For hard copy print of books, please contact Dr. Fey at RCI, P.O. Box C, Ironia, NJ 07845 or eMail: Feyms@aol.com.

Hard copy books are also available at *The Institute for Silver Dollar Education and Research*, at website: *Ilovesilver dollars.org* or by contacting Executive Director John Baumgart at John.Baumgart@comcast.net

Amazon Kindle

Fey, Michael S. 2019. *The Complete Virtual Guide to Pricing Your Morgan Silver Dollars.* 286 pp. RCI

Van Allen, Leroy, & A. George Mallis. 2023. *Part I or II or III of Three. Comprehensive Catalog and Encyclopedia or Morgan & Peace Dollars.* RCI Total 520 pp.

Leroy Van Allen. 2011. *Wonders of Morgan Dollars.* 139 pp. RCI

Leroy Van Allen. 2013. *Wonders of Peace Dollars.* 273 pp. RCI

Leroy Van Allen. 2006. *Morgan Dollars 8 & 7 Over 8 Tail Feather Story.* 52 pp. RCI

Leroy Van Allen. 2010. *1878 P 7 Tail Feather Morgan Dollar Attribution Guide.* 130 pp. RCI

Leroy Van Allen. 2006. *1878 S Morgan Dollar Attribution Guide.* 139 pp. RCI

Fey, Michael S. 2009 The Top 100 Morgan Dollar Varieties: The VAM Keys

FURTHER REFERENCES

Hard Copy Books

Fey, Michael S. 2019. The Top 100 Morgan Dollar Varieties: The VAM Keys. 286 pp. RCI

Fey, Michael S. 2008. *A Decade of Top 100 Insights*. RCI 174 pp.

Van Allen, Leroy. 1991. *RotaFlip Die Rotation Booklet and Guide*. 1991. RCI

Kimpton, M.D., Mark. 2005. *Elite Clashed Morgan Dollars*. RCI 160 pp

Van Allen, Leroy, & A. George Mallis. 2023. *Comprehensive Catalog and Encyclopedia or Morgan & Peace Dollars*. RCI Total 520 pp.

Van Allen, Leroy 2011. *Wonders of Morgan Dollars*. 139 pp. RCI

Van Allen, Leroy 2013. *Wonders of Peace Dollars*. 273 pp. RCI

Van Allen, Leroy 2006. *Morgan Dollars 8 & 7 Over 8 Tail Feather Story*. 52 pp. RCI

Van Allen, Leroy 2010. *1878 P 7 Tail Feather Morgan Dollar Attribution Guide*. 130 pp. RCI

Van Allen, Leroy 2006. *1878 S Morgan Dollar Attribution Guide*. 139 pp. RCI

Van Allen, Leroy 2013. *Die Gouges and Scratches Peace Dollar Attribution Guide*. *109 pp* RCI

Van Allen, Leroy 2008. *1921 Scribbles Morgan Dollar Attribution Guide*. 234 pp. RCI

Van Allen, Leroy. 2013. *Misplaced Date Digits Morgan Dollar Attribution Guide*. 57 pp RCI

Van Allen, Leroy. 2017. *Dashed Under 8 Morgan Dollar Attribution Guide*. 53 pp. RCI

Van Allen, Leroy. 2009. *Overdates and Over Mint Marks of Morgan Dollar Attribution Guide*. 53 pp. RCI

Van Allen, Leroy. 2015. *Denticle & Die Impressions Morgan Dollar Attribution Guide*. 109 pp. RCI

Van Allen, Leroy. 2009. *1921 P Infrequently Reeded or Wide Reeding Morgan Dollar Attribution Guide*. 31 pp. RCI

Van Allen, Leroy. 2011 *Amazing Changing 1921 S VAM 1B Thorn Head Morgan Dollar*. 2011. 22 pp. RCI

Van Allen, Leroy. 2009. *1889 P Doubled Ear Morgan Dollar Attribution Guide*. 32 pp. RCI

Van Allen, Leroy. 2016. *Micro o and Other Counterfeit Morgan and Peace Dollars*. 191 pp RCI

Van Allen, Leroy. 2005. *Micro o Mint Mark on Morgan Dollars*. 32 pp. RCI

Van Allen, Leroy. 2005. *Die Markers for 1921 Morgan and Peace Proof Dollars*. 9 pp. RCI

Van Allen, Leroy and Baumgart, John. 1992-Date Various VAM Book Yearly Supplements. RCI